C000127456

 CHRIS SAVORY has spent l to make the world a bette local politics, education, co volunteering for social enterprises. He was born in 1961 in Kitwe, Northern Rhodesia. He arrived in England aged two and has subsequently lived in Kent, Essex, Paris, Oxfordshire, Missouri, Yorkshire, Berwickshire, Herefordshire, Dorset and South-West London. Chris is married with two adult stepchildren. He loves his ukulele, choirs, watching football, rivers, soft toys, marmalade, the seaside, beer, country music and London. He struggles with chronic depression, exhaustion and joint pains.

0522

CONFESSIONS OF A NON-VIOLENT REVOLUTIONARY

BEAN STEW, BLISTERS, BLOCKADES AND BENDERS
THE TRUE STORY OF A PEACE ACTIVIST IN
THATCHER'S BRITAIN

CHRIS SAVORY

CLAIRVIEW

Clairview Books Ltd.,
Russet, Sandy Lane,
West Hoathly,
W. Sussex RH19 4QQ

www.clairviewbooks.com

Published by Clairview Books 2020

Figs. 2, 7, 18, 19 by Margie Barbour; figs. 10, 11 by John Brierly; figs. 12 by Amanda; fig. 14 from *Ripon Gazette*. All other images are from the author's private collection. Every effort has been made to identify copyright holders. The publishers will be happy to correct any omissions in future editions

A CIP catalogue record for this book is available from the British Library

ISBN 978 1 912992 14 0

Cover by Morgan Creative
Typeset by Symbiosys Technologies, Visakhapatnam, India
Printed and bound by 4Edge Ltd, Essex

Contents

Foreword

This book is a personal account based on my memory and some records I have kept since the early 1980s. I was living an uncluttered and peripatetic life, with no thought at the time that I would one day like to write an account of these extraordinary years – so the actual records are patchy. I lost contact with most of the people in this book long ago, and so I have changed most names to protect identities. I have used dialogue sparingly and the conversations are not an exact record, but my best attempt to convey the meaning and feelings of the moment. The photographs were mostly given to me at the time by fellow activists and are credited where possible.

I would like to thank my excellent writing tutor Mark McCrum and my memoir-writing mates, Cas Bulmer, Paul Davies and Kate McCarey for their invaluable support. Thanks to Katrin Williams who made a huge contribution in helping me trim and focus the manuscript and to Jenni Mills for some early editorial support. Thanks to my friends Catriona Gilmour-Hamilton, Ian Bray and Simon Garwood for reading early drafts and giving helpful feedback. Special thanks to Sevak Gulbekian of Clairview Books for believing in this project. Thanks to my Dad for financial help at important times, and finally, a huge thank you to my wife Margie Barbour for 25 years of love, support and friendship, and helping me through the dark times.

This book is dedicated to non-violent activists all over the world who are currently trying to make our world a better place. Thank you.

Chris Savory
January 2020

Preface

The 4,000-mile peace march from Los Angeles to New York and the 1982 UN special session on disarmament was over. The Buddhist monks who had led the way said goodbye and flew back to Japan. Other marchers went straight back to their jobs and families. The freer and more politically-radical of us stayed on to extend the protest here in the Big Apple. About thirty of us crammed into a basement apartment in Greenwich Village, belonging to the happily named George Bliss, for a day of preparation and a nervous night's sleep, sprawled together in our sleeping bags like caterpillar chrysalises. In the morning I got up early, hugged as many of my friends as I could, and set off to take the subway to Lexington and 53rd Street.

This was my first large-scale 'direct action'. More than 1,000 peace campaigners had pledged to blockade the UN missions of the five nuclear-armed powers. In my honour our little group went to the British mission on Third Avenue. I was with my best friends from the World Peace March, Matt and Juli, together with half a dozen fellow activists from their hometown of Columbus Ohio. As a foreigner who risked deportation, I was a support person for the affinity group. The conversation bounced back and forth between the Columbus crew.

'Do you think we'll get arrested?'

'What if they just let us sit – how long before you need to pee out some of that coffee Sean?'

'Has anyone been in Rikers Island?'

'I need to be back at work on Wednesday'

'Hey Chris, what the fuck are the Brits doing with nukes anyway?'

It was crowded as we emerged from the warm, smelly safety of the subway. I wasn't used to the feeling of being hemmed in by skyscrapers. There were police everywhere, standing solid with big bellies straining at leather belts, hands on hips, near the baton and the gun. We split up to get around the wooden barricades. Down a side street

Fig. 1. My handbook for the action

I saw dozens of police vans including a bus full of helmeted riot police. The blockaders regrouped and sat straight down in the middle of the road. I loved these beautiful people, these clever, funny, compassionate, angry, determined people: my people, my friends.

I felt an unexpected joy, a sense of possibility that we could make the politicians sit up and take notice, as well as intense pride at being part of this great principled movement for humanity. But as the police arrived, two for each demonstrator, and started to drag them roughly across the street, my guts hit my throat. That's when I started singing; singing for all I was worth, singing for peace, singing for justice, singing for my life.

'We shall overcome, We shall overcome, We shall overcome some day...', I bellowed, out of tune but with every fibre of my being.

3

1
Bike Ride to Freedom

My life as a full-time, unpaid, roving would-be non-violent revolutionary had begun twelve months earlier. On a sunny June morning in 1981, I had woken up in my Gran's house in Cowley, Oxford. I pulled back the thin brown curtains and looked through the bars that Grandad had put up to stop curious grandchildren falling out of this first-floor window. My eyes took in the familiar lichen-patina of the sun-lounge roof with its peeling yellow woodwork, the coal bunker, the ugly concrete-grey garage and the rickety garden shed. These objects were comforting, like the old, single, metal-framed bed with its dusty pink-paisley patterned eiderdown. I scanned the garden, the vegetable patch I'd been cultivating, the lawn I'd been mowing and the four apple trees that had survived since the 1930s, then I gazed beyond the green wire fence across Morris Motor's cricket pitch and bowling green to one of the iconic panoramas of England – the Dreaming Spires of Oxford. I opened the window and drank in the soft, soporific air. I loved being here, at 159 Hollow Way. This house felt like home because it was where I experienced unconditional love and acceptance. It's where I basked in the rock-solid glow of Granny Ross's approval.

She was downstairs and as I opened the sliding door into the narrow kitchen, she passed me a mug of strong tea, her knobbly and knotted arthritic hands shaking from incipient Parkinson's disease.

'Here you are, love, how are you feeling?'

'All right, thanks Gran, but better when the exams are over'.

I smiled as the lie tripped so easily from my lips that I half believed it myself, but I wasn't really all right at all. I was confused, angry, scared, and lonely. I was trying to find the courage to turn my back on the opportunity of a lifetime in order to attempt to save the world from nuclear destruction and ecological catastrophe. My year-long part-time activism no longer seemed enough. The crisis felt so acute that I wanted to devote all my energies to averting it.

For the last few weeks of the summer term in 1981, I had abandoned my spartan room at Lady Margaret Hall and come to stay with my Gran in Cowley so that I could revise better for the exams, without interruptions, and enjoy the TLC that Gran specialised in. In the middle of the summer term, I had asked the college authorities if I could take a year out of my studies as I was not making the best use of my time at Oxford and needed to find my motivation again. They weren't enthusiastic but agreed.

The revising was finally over and I had one more exam to take. The night before had been wretched. I had been good at exams, but I no longer believed that this meant anything. I felt like a performing exam-monkey, working hard to get the 'peanut' reward of a good grade: but what use were those peanut-grades in the face of the agonies and injustices of the world? Would my sixteen O-levels protect me from a nuclear attack?

I wheeled my bike out of the garage, tucked my shiny, charity-shop suit trousers into my black socks, stuck the mortarboard under a bungee on the rear rack, and set off downhill, my commoners' gown flapping behind me. I rode past the gates of the car factory where my Grandad had toiled for thirty years. He was the bastard child of a servant from West Oxfordshire farm-labouring stock. Grandad lied about his age to join the Grenadier Guards at seventeen, luckily just too late to see any action in the war. He got a job at Pressed Steel (the Morris Motor's body plant) in the late 1920s because the boss recognised his Guards' tie. He hung on to the job through the Great Depression, despite the soul-destroying rigours of the assembly line and finally the ulcers that the hard work and years of poor diet had given him.

After his third child, my Mum, was born in 1931 in a small rented flat above a shop on the Cowley Road, Grandad volunteered for the works fire service and was rewarded in 1934 by being given the chance to buy a house close to the factory for £150 (about the same as a year's wages). It was from this house – originally a two-up two-down with no indoor toilet, hot water or heating, but now extended and modernised – that I had started my journey.

I cycled on past the vast factory buildings and continued pedalling down the Oxford Road, past the Swan pub, on through the Cowley Marsh, past the allotments, the cinema turned Bingo Hall, and then past the flat where my Mum was born. I was feeling very emotional, biting back a few tears. Grandad would have been proud of me if he were still alive. Mum and Gran were proud of me, but the trouble was I couldn't feel proud of myself. I knew they would be shocked and upset if I didn't stay and finish my degree. I knew I'd be letting them down, but it was difficult for me to see how I could comfortably take that step with the world in such a mess.

At the bottom of the Cowley Road was EOA Books, run by my friend Jon from the Ecology Party. This was where I got all my political magazines, books, pamphlets and information about local events. Everything changed as I cycled over Magdalen Bridge. The Georgian splendour of Magdalen College, with its gracious rooms and private deer park was a potent symbol of the long-lasting privileges of the ruling class. These were the people with power and wealth who seemed to me to be oblivious to the threats posed by the escalating nuclear arms race, the prospect of ecological disaster and the sufferings of the increasing number of unemployed and poor.

I knew from my experience of a year at Oxford that it was unlikely that I'd get into that class proper, just simply from studying at the university. I didn't have the right family background or contacts. Not like my college-mates, Raymona and Nigella, both girls named after their self-important fathers, Ray Horrocks, managing director of British Leyland, and Nigel Lawson, cabinet minister and soon to be Chancellor of the Exchequer. Or for that matter, the many other sons and daughters of the landed, titled and wealthy that I mixed with every day, but who mostly looked straight through me. One time, when I had just returned from digging my Gran's vegetable garden wearing donkey jacket and boots, a cut-glass accent stopped me and asked me if I was a gardener at the college, as there was some litter by the boat-sheds that needed clearing up. I only managed a muttered, 'I'm a bloody student here too', as I slunk away, feeling out of place and powerless in the face of such casual entitlement. These angry thoughts broke my concentration and I almost fell off my bike at the lights halfway up the High Street as a white van cut me up. The passenger lent out of the window and shouted:

'Where's your Batmobile, dickhead?' (a reference to my academic gown).

No, I thought, gathering my breath and dignity as I rested at the red lights, I'll never be a pukka member of the ruling class, but I'm definitely in line to becoming a trusty lieutenant – a senior civil servant perhaps or a corporate senior manager, high-ranking banker, economist or accountant. There was no longer an empire to run but a new Thatcherite paradise to create, with rich rewards for those at the top and for those who helped keep them there.

I was hoping to find a different path – a way of using my talents for the good of the world. After these exams I would be free to pursue my dreams. It was to give myself some time to find this new path that I had asked to take a year out of my studies. What would freedom taste like, though? Would I even recognise it when I saw it, smelt it, touched it? I didn't feel free as I locked my bike up and entered the exam-halls on Oxford High Street. This was the final exam, and it was Politics. I liked this subject and I'd worked hard. That afternoon I was given a gift. The paper was on Political Ideologies and there was a juicy plum on Anarchism. As I bit into it with relish, writing with passion and knowledge, I knew I had this one in the bag.

Outside, when it was all over, I crossed the road and joined some friends outside The Queen's College, swigging champagne from a bottle to celebrate. We crowded the pavement and spilt on to the road, a horde of happy, black-and-white suited penguins, raucous and high with the relief of finishing a gruelling set of exams. The sour-faced Bulldogs, the university police, in their dark suits and bowler hats, snapped, snarled and scowled at us. They wanted us off the public streets and out of the gaze of the 'town'.

As we walked back through the university parks to our college, our caged energy was released in a bout of cub-wrestling and mortarboard frisbee. I damaged my best friend Sam's mortarboard and he was genuinely pissed-off as he had borrowed it from another friend.

'Have mine – I'm never going to wear this piece of crap again.'

We arrived back at Lady Margaret Hall and joined a party in someone's room. I drank to obliterate, rather than celebrate. At one point I found myself curled up under the desk snogging a fellow student – and rebel – Karen. We were friends but there was no real spark between us. I was contemplating leaving Oxford and she was about to fail her exams, but at least we were young, warm, sentient beings who could enjoy physical intimacy. Then I went back alone to my bare college room to take off the gown and sleep off the drink.

Hunger drove me to get up and leave this comfortless room for the last time. Was this freedom? I walked back to the High Street and bought a large portion of soggy, lukewarm chips to eat as I walked slowly down the road to my locked bike. It was more than three miles home, uphill much of the way. When I got back, Gran had already gone to bed. Freedom tasted sour: salt, vinegar and loneliness.

2
Brave New World?

Day one of my new career as a non-violent revolutionary began late and groggy. I pottered in the garden and dozed with Gran in the sun-lounge and later in front of Coronation Street. Day two was much the same. I had set my life on a new course only to become becalmed by a lack of knowledge and information. I grappled with the tricky question of how, exactly, to bring about world peace and create an ecological utopia? There were no self-help guides in the bookshops, no *Non-Violent Revolution Made Easy* or *Teach Yourself Eco-Socialism*, among the copious self-improvement tomes. I didn't have a Pope or a Party to tell me what to do, and there was no Google or Wikipedia. What I did have, however, were two magazines: *Peace News* and the *Ecologist*.

In pre-Internet days such magazines and the shops that sold them were the lifeblood of counter-cultural movements. I pored over the small ads for inspiration and was intrigued by an advert for communal living. A straight nuclear family had felt like an emotional prison for the older-teenage me. Mum didn't like my girlfriends, or my drinking.

I had met Clare at a party in February 1979 and asked her out straight away. She lived in Chelmsford, about half a mile further out of town than us, and went to a convent school in Brentwood. She would often call in on her long walk home from the station. One day, after I'd kissed her goodbye outside the back door, I came back into the lounge to find my Mum with a sour, pinched-lip expression.

'If she must come here so often tell her to be less obvious,' she said.

'What on earth are you talking about, Mum?'

'You know very well – lying on the sofa showing everything she's got.'

'For God's sake Mum, you're being weird,' was all I could muster in response.

Dad enforced a strict home-by-11pm rule, even when I was eighteen and in the sixth form.

One night I came home later than Dad had demanded, disturbing his much-needed sleep.

'While you're still living under my roof you live by my rules,' he said as he emerged from his bedroom.

He stared angrily through drooping eyelids, his Desperate Dan chin jutting out with fierce stubble – but incongruous in dark-red, neatly-ironed pyjamas. 'I'm nearly nineteen for god's sake – it's not even midnight. Have you any idea how unreasonable you're being.'

'I said home by eleven o'clock and when I say eleven o'clock, I mean eleven o'clock, not a quarter to twelve.'

I balled my fists, standing at the top of the stairs, shaking a little as the impotent rage, beer and testosterone swirled around. My internal monologue went something like this: I've always worked hard at school, never got into trouble with the teachers, I don't do drugs, I play sport, I'm a prefect, I've got into Oxford, I keep out of trouble in town, I earn money where I can – so why the fucking hell can't you cut me some slack? A lifetime of being afraid to stand up to the righteousness of Dad's cast-iron certainty and the unwavering implementation of his rules, backed up by hefty slaps to the head or the slipper for serious transgressions, made confrontation too difficult for me and so I whined,

'It's not late – it's Friday night. We left the pub before anybody else and you know it takes time to walk Clare home.'

'I'm not having it – come back by eleven or don't go out.'

I really wanted to hit him, to assert my manhood, but we both knew that wasn't going to happen. Dad was definitely King of our Castle.

I wondered if communal living would be a better way. Down with nuclear families, as well as nuclear bombs!

Practical work appealed to me, after all the studying and exams. Working with my hands seemed more honest and more directly useful than discussing old theories over sherry with my tutors. This was my own personal cultural revolution – thinking that it was a good idea for intellectuals to taste the glorious sweat and toil of the peasantry.

In the end I sent off three letters, all resplendent with the 'Nuclear Power, No Thanks!' smiley sun on the envelope re-use stickers. One was for the British Trust for Conservation Volunteers (BTCV) brochure, one was to join WWOOF (working weekends on organic farms) and one was to the Teachers commune in North Wales.

I spent a week in hope and expectation that something life-changing was coming through the letterbox. I had to weather the disappointment of no-post days, but then I revelled in the glory of a fat envelope flopping on to the cracked, black and yellow lino of Gran's tiny hall.

The BTCV had paid staff, and so their brochure was the first to arrive. I made a cup of tea, took it out into the garden, constructed a rather wonky roll-up and slowly read and re-read the lists of two-week conservation task working holidays. I chose dry-stone walling in the Lake District and footpath repair in Snowdonia. I filled in the form, wrote a cheque and sent it back in the post.

The reply from the Teachers arrived two days later and included a pamphlet extolling the virtues of communal living and a letter to say that I would be welcome as long as I stayed for a minimum of five days and was prepared to work for my keep. By mid-July I had my summer worked out. I had booked the two conservation tasks, a visit to the commune, the Ecology Party summer gathering, and a couple of WWOOF-ing weekends. This was all topped off with a fortnight in Germany with my now long-standing girlfriend, Clare, who was spending the summer in Cologne as an au pair.

The summer started perfectly with two weeks camping and working outdoors in the sunshine in Langdale, where I discovered the satisfaction of finding just the right shaped stone to secure a new chunk of wall. On my day off I climbed Langdale Pike. I strode up the short bouncy turf and patches of grey rock and scree. After a couple of hours, I reached a black mountain tarn fed by a small waterfall. I was alone and didn't hesitate to strip off and enjoy a crisp, cold dip. I ate my cheese-and-pickle sandwiches and lay on my back, entranced by the wispy clouds and the distant song of the skylarks. I read several chapters of the book I had carried with me, *Dharma Bums* by Jack Kerouac. I felt like a modern-day Japhy Ryder, at one with nature, free and pure. I had been anxious about the future at the start of the summer, but now felt energised and optimistic. We *can* change the world!

A week later, I took the train from Oxford to Bangor and then a taxi up to the Teachers' communal farm, which was about two miles up into the hills. The welcome was cordial, and after a basic lunch I was put to work straight away creosoting fences. My 'room' in the attic of a barn had a folding bed made up with clean sheets, and a battered bedside table and chair.

It transpired that both David and Linda, the leaders of this self-described 'democratic community based on consensus decision-making', were away. The commune was funded by work in computer software design, carried out from a shared house in the home counties. David and Linda spent their time split between the two sites. The permanent residents of the farm were two men and a woman in their late twenties, who, it seemed, were at the bottom of the hierarchy. Working with them for a few days around the gardens and outbuildings, I was reminded of rabbits caught in headlights. They were very careful not to say anything negative about the setup.

On the third evening we were joined at supper by the leaders.

'I'll have my supper now', Linda ordered. One of the rabbits jumped up and bustled about in the kitchen, not even getting a thank you when he put down a plate of hot food.

After supper, David questioned me on my interests and intentions. I told him I'd finished a year at Oxford and was unhappy with the course and the people there, and so had taken a year out to explore alternative ways of living.

'You'll probably be like the rest of the students who visit us, playing around for a year and then going back to university. You'll finish your degree, get yourself a job and a wife and have a family and never dare to live differently, I bet. We see it all the time.'

I burbled protestations in response to the attack, but it stayed with me as I lay awake on the camp bed that night. I didn't like this place. It was creepy. The underlings seemed frightened and the leaders arrogant. Maybe family life wasn't so bad after all, if this was the alternative. The Teachers were certainly well-organised and worked hard, not lazy hippies, despite the preponderance of long hair and beards, and David was clearly clever. He had pricked my pride and found my weak spot very quickly. I was highly sensitive to the charge of not being serious about wanting to live a different life and to change the world.

I was influenced by David of the Teachers much more than I should have been. His dismissiveness strengthened my resolve not to return to Oxford, but to commit myself fully to change. The last thing I wanted was to be a champagne socialist, a demo-dilettante, a smug middle-class intellectual, the kind of person my Dad hated most in the world. I had heard enough tea-time diatribes against do-gooding Hampstead trendies (like Lord Longford), union leaders and Labour politicians who lined their own pockets whilst espousing socialism, to know that Dad thought they were the worst kind of hypocrites – and I agreed. After all, we were cut from the same fiercely-independent, aspirational working class/lower middle-class, non-conformist, Protestant cloth. My Dad's dad was the son of a railway ticket collector from Peterborough, who died young. My Grandad had to abandon a promising school career and go to work at fourteen. Both my Dad and his elder brother won scholarships to the local Grammar school and, later, scholarships to Oxford University. All of this had been achieved without any outside help but through individual effort, delayed gratification and respectability. My Dad never developed a religious faith, but he inherited a fierce Calvinist morality and work ethic, which perhaps goes back to our ancestors who came to East Anglia in the seventeenth century – they were Huguenots escaping religious persecution in France.

Like my Dad, I have this legacy of Protestantism stamped through me like a stick of rock, in orange letters of course! There are no half-measures in this ideology. You are either saved or damned. There are no shades of grey: right is right and wrong is wrong. It's not so surprising, then, that I didn't want to just play at being a peace activist whilst I was a student and then settle down to a normal job, career and family, as most people took great delight in predicting that I would. I felt impelled to walk the walk as well as talk the talk.

3
On the Eve of Destruction

It turned out that I was just the right age to be drawn into the movement for nuclear disarmament. In the spring of 1961, Dad was into his fifth year of seven as a forest officer in Northern Rhodesia (now Zambia) and my mum had been confined to hospital at six months' pregnant with seriously high blood pressure. Six weeks before her due date, she bled alarmingly, and I was whisked out. I was alone in an incubator, whilst Mum's life hung in the balance. Back home from the hospital, I spent many months crying with all my tiny might, inconsolable. I was shocked rigid by this sudden, brutal and unexpected entrance into the world of four glass walls, tubes and no mother's touch. Mum often locked the door of my room because she couldn't bear her inability to stop me crying. My older brother Pete, already enraged by his Mum's lengthy absence, experienced severe sibling jealousy when the tiny usurper returned home with Mum.

In the wider world, in the year of my birth, John Kennedy had become president of the USA and tried to invade Cuba. The United States tested its first Minuteman I intercontinental ballistic missile and the Soviet Union fired a 50-megaton hydrogen bomb, making the biggest explosion in history. The Russians put the first man in space and built the Berlin Wall. President Kennedy advised American families to build bomb shelters and the first US troops and helicopters were sent to Vietnam. The Cold War had dramatically intensified.

I developed an interest in current affairs as a teenager, which I read about in the family copies of the *Daily Telegraph* and *Sunday Express* and watched on the nine o'clock news on the BBC. Up to the age of seventeen I broadly accepted my parents' conservative view of the world and had no contact with alternative views. However, the drip, drip, drip of news items about nuclear testing (there were at least twenty-three separate tests between August and December 1978 by five different countries), the arms race and concerns about global nuclear proliferation were having an impact on me.

At some point during the autumn of 1978 I drew a cartoon of sorts. It showed a stick man, who was obviously blind, with an H-bomb on his head walking towards Golgotha – where Jesus and the two thieves were being crucified. I then put it in a drawer without telling anyone about my obvious anxieties about the future.

By 1979, as I turned eighteen, the Soviet Union had finally caught up with, and then overtaken, the USA in the nuclear arms race, with both countries holding around 30,000 warheads (1,600 was considered more than enough to wipe each other off the face of the earth). Margaret Thatcher's new government pledged to replace Britain's Polaris nuclear-armed submarines with the much more powerful Trident system. President Carter responded to German fears over the siting of Soviet SS20 missiles in Eastern Europe by agreeing to station 562 Cruise and Pershing missiles in West Germany and the United Kingdom.

My activism emerged from a deep and genuine fear of nuclear holocaust. I had abandonment issues from my birth experience which were reinforced by events later in childhood, and I think that the threat posed by nuclear weapons to our very existence hit me especially hard because – unconsciously at the time – they resonated with my personal feelings of insecurity and anxiety.

My use of Christian imagery in the drawing was significant. I had been sent to Sunday school and Church aged five and onwards, had been confirmed at twelve, with a feeling of genuine faith, and studied Matthew's Gospel in depth for Religious Education O-level at fourteen. We had Christian assemblies every day at school. Jesus's teaching in the Sermon on the Mount is unequivocal about peace and forgiveness and I had been profoundly influenced by it.

I had grown up in a conservative family and grammar school environment full of certainty and rigid views: individual agency was the key to understanding the world; people have free-will and the capacity to make practical and moral choices; hard work and righteousness are the key to successfully climbing the social pyramid; the poor are essentially to blame for their poverty, whether this be individuals or nations. Stephen, one of the ragged boys in my year at Junior School, fainted in assembly due to lack of food and my Mum was outraged later that week when she saw Mrs Flynn in the corner shop buying expensive, new-fangled mousse deserts for her five children.

The worldview I was immersed in went something like this: Communism hasn't worked because it goes against human nature, all forms of socialism are delusional (and the Labour Party are Socialists) and Catholicism is evil. Go to church, but don't get enthusiastic about religion. Apartheid in South Africa and white rule in Rhodesia are right because it is the whites who kept the farms working and the economy going. Trades unions are wrong because extremists take over and use intimidation to force workers to strike. You should rely on your own efforts to get on. Martin Luther King was an ungrateful extremist. Politics should be kept out of sport. The IRA are animals. The Yanks had treated us appallingly over Suez, and they were not to be trusted. The French couldn't stand up for themselves and needed us to save them from the Germans. We won the war – and look how we've been treated since and how Germany and Japan have been given such a leg up. No sex before marriage. Homosexuality is abhorrent and perverse. Drugs are wrong; don't gamble and only drink in moderation. Polish your shoes every day and keep your hair with short back and sides. A woman's primary role is to look after the family. Competition is good, and you get what you deserve in life. Keep charity at home for our own kind. Respect your elders and betters, be proud and grateful to be British. We need a strong military to defend our way of life at home and around the world. The Soviet Union want to invade the West and turn us all into Communists. Nuclear weapons are a necessary evil.

The trouble with being brought up with such rigid certainty is that when cracks appear in the framework of beliefs (preparing for nuclear war is the best way to achieve peace, for example), there is a danger of the dam bursting. And with very little warning for me, or those around me, a trickle of questioning in my eighteenth year, became a torrent before I was nineteen, and then very soon the dam was smashed to pieces.

One Saturday morning in May 1980 I walked into Chelmsford town centre with some birthday money in search of bargain records. As I approached the central square of the concrete shopping precinct with its sad, litter-strewn fountain, I spotted several tables full of posters, banners and literature. The stall, it transpired, was promoting the Campaign for Nuclear Disarmament (CND). I approached

Fig 2. My CND badges

the first table and picked up a leaflet about the effects of a nuclear bomb exploding on Chelmsford and soon one of the stall holders, a jolly looking man with a flushed face and silver glasses, asked me if I was interested in joining CND. He was a Labour Party stalwart and veteran of the Aldermaston marches in the early 1960s. I stayed and talked with him and the other two helpers for about twenty minutes and left clutching a great pile of literature and my first CND badge: the classic symbol, white on a black background. The group had set up their stall to publicise the launch of a new CND branch in the town with a showing of the previously banned film *The War Game*. This meeting was held in the basement of the town library. It was packed for the occasion with well over one hundred people crammed into the room with some overflowing into the corridor. We heard inspiring and passionate speeches from people who had been involved in the first wave of protests against nuclear weapons in the late 1950s and early 1960s. In particular, I was fired-up by a local artist, resplendent with long grey hair and a wispy beard, called Jimmy Johns, who had been on all of the Aldermaston marches and had been part of the civil-disobedience campaign of the 'Committee of 100'[1]. It was just so bloody exciting to realise that even in an ordinary town like Chelmsford so many other people were thinking the same way. I paid my sub and became a member of CND.

I plunged straight into writing for and delivering the branch newsletter, and going to all the meetings. I took part in the first protests. My first demonstration was in June 1980 at RAF Molesworth. We went in cars because the group was so new and there was no time to hire a coach. The decision to put American cruise missiles at Greenham Common and Molesworth had just been announced and as we were in Chelmsford, in the Eastern region, we went to Molesworth near Cambridge.

I spent an uncomfortable two hours squashed in the back of a Ford Cortina with two middle-aged CND-ers. The journey was made bearable because we had Jimmy Johns in the front passenger seat, regaling us with stories of the Aldermaston marches and the sit-down protests in London. The actual demo wasn't really a demo at all. We eventually arrived at a deserted base, drove around for a while, stopped to stretch our legs, and came home – a truly unglamorous start to my peace protesting career.

The first big march that I went on was on Sunday 22 June 1980, in the middle of my 'A'-level exams. It was organised by the Labour Party and we walked along the South Bank to a rally in Hyde Park. It rained all afternoon, but it felt great to be part of such a large group of people who believed that we needed to change the world for the better. There were trades unionists carrying their proud, colourful banners full of inspiring slogans and stories. There were Trotskyists with multitudinous aggressive placards and newspapers. There were groups of sensibly shod Quakers, whole families with toddlers in pushchairs and branches of the Labour Party from all over the country.

---

[1] The Committee of 100 would gather a minimum of 100 people committed to taking illegal action. When they had the required number signed up, they staged sit-down protests, often in central London, to initiate mass-arrests and trials to gain maximum publicity.

Never underestimate the power of demonstrations to inspire people – like me in 1980 – who are on their first political march. You see that you are not alone, as you grab carrier bags full of papers and leaflets and badges to take home like a hoard of treasure. You remember the chants, songs and sense of comradeship. And, just like your first dive off the high board, now that you have found the courage to do it once, you can't wait to do it again.

The first national CND demonstration since the 1960s was held in London on 26 October 1980, under the slogan 'Protest and Survive'. This was a re-working of the government's civil defence pamphlet 'Protect and Survive', which included gems of advice on how to survive a nuclear attack by hiding under the kitchen table. There were over 100,000 people on the march and, as I arrived in Trafalgar Square, it was already crammed to bursting on all sides. Those around me shuffled forward, encouraging those in front of us to get a bit cosier with the people in front of them, as there were plenty of others still arriving at our backs. The speeches had been going on for some time and, as I approached the square, I heard indecipherable station-announcer type voices followed by ragged cheers. I was now close enough to see the podium under Nelson's column. A new speaker was taking the microphone and I could just make out a mane of white hair, which was regularly swept back with a great flourish. It was Edward (E.P.) Thompson, the Marxist historian and founder of the European Nuclear Disarmament movement. I couldn't make out all the words, but he implored us over and over again to: 'Feel Your Strength'. His words echoed and rippled through the air, spreading a surge of determination and encouragement through us all. The people were on the move and we *would* overcome some day.

I went back to Oxford, full of energy and enthusiasm for the disarmament cause, and threw myself into action with Campaign Atom (CATOM), the Oxford CND group: leafleting, writing letters, getting petitions signed, taking part in vigils in the city centre. On 25 February, I went to the inaugural meeting of the Campaign Atom Direct Action Group. I was already thinking that our normal democratic channels were not working fast enough in the face of impending nuclear war. During the last Labour government, Prime Minister James Callaghan and three senior colleagues had secretly agreed a major update of Britain's Polaris submarine-based missile system. Now we had the newly-elected, gung-ho President Reagan in the

White House to go alongside our own Mrs Thatcher. There didn't seem to be any room for voices for peace and disarmament in government. Opposition voices in January 1981 were split too, as Roy Jenkins, Shirley Williams, David Owen and Bill Rodgers announced their plan to leave Labour and form a new party, which became the Social Democratic Party (SDP), citing as a key reason their commitment to keeping British nuclear weapons.

The Direct-Action group meeting was memorable because I saw Rip Bulkley for the first time – a Trotskyist intellectual who was also exceptionally tall and a persuasive speaker. About a dozen of us met in a gloomy back room of the East Oxford Community Centre and were full of wild ideas and imaginings of revolution. In the end, our modest plans to occupy a local bunker petered out, and our first action was limited to some tame street theatre. Not quite the storming of the Winter Palace, and the government could still sleep easy!

My political education came mostly from speakers, discussions and pamphlets rather than books. I attended ten peace movement meetings that February including talks from an East German newspaper reporter and E.P. Thompson from the European Campaign for Nuclear Disarmament, who had inspired us at the national CND rally in October.

There was a strong European perspective to our campaigning at this time, and one of the few student-led initiatives at Oxford was to attend a conference and demonstration at the NATO headquarters in Brussels, at Easter 1980, focussing on de-militarising the whole of Europe. I had quickly made friends with the small group of 'lefties' in my college. The second years doing Philosophy, Politics and Economics (PPE) included Richard (who went on to become a Labour MP) and glamorous and funny Sarian from South Wales, who were very supportive of us newcomers and delighted to have some reinforcements. In my year the PPE students were less political, and I teamed up with two English students: tall, blond, man of the world, Sam (whose mortar board I later damaged) and fiery Welsh redhead, Phil. In the spring term at college, Sam, Phil and I as well as a first-year maths student, Karen, had got into the habit of staying up most of the night. Sam had the best room – in fact, rooms – as there was a sitting room as well as a bedroom. Sam also had the best record collection, the most money and the best connections to buy hashish. So, we mostly ended up in his room, talking, smoking and listening to Patti Smith, Crosby Stills Nash & Young and Bob Dylan.

Towards the end of the Spring term, Sam, Phil, Sarian and I booked a place on a coach to Brussels organised by Gordon from Students Against Nuclear Energy (SANE). We pulled out of Oxford mid-morning on the way to London. Our party was made up of the four of us from LMH, Gordon and his gang of about a dozen. In addition were four smartly dressed, middle-aged Asians. We drove through central London in order to pick up a contingent of Scottish students who had travelled overnight on the train from Dundee to King's Cross. They had clearly not slept overnight and had been drinking steadily. I never did discover if they were genuinely anti-nuclear or whether they just fancied a cheap Easter holiday.

We eventually left the traffic jams of London behind and reached Dover in time for the ferry to Calais. It was a small boat by today's standards and the sea was choppy with a sizeable swell. I preferred to be on deck in the fresh air, so I was standing looking out to sea, chatting to Phil and trying not to feel seasick. Something must have caught the corner of my eye, making me glance to the left. What I saw was a great orange arc of what I thought initially to be mashed swede, swirling in the wind towards us. I was transfixed by the beauty of this spectacle, and my mind was slow to connect it to our heavy-drinking Scottish pals on the other side of the boat. Phil was quicker on the uptake and pulled me to one side, too late to save me from getting flecked with vomit on my one and only set of clothes.

The next issue was at passport control, where we were held for at least an hour after our passports had been taken away by the officials. Then four uniformed men arrived, bundled the middle-aged Asians away and gave us our passports back.

It was now evening as we drove off to Brussels. We were close to our destination when we stopped for a comfort break at a small service station after midnight. Gordon rang the organisers to find out where exactly we should go, to be told that because he hadn't booked in through the official channel, we didn't have anywhere to sleep. Good old Gordon. We then had to wait for three or four hours until an organiser came out to guide us to our destination. We eventually got a couple of hours on a gym floor after some Italians had been hustled out early to allow us to have a turn.

Later in the morning we gathered in a square somewhere in Brussels. It was cobbled and surrounded by higgledy-piggledy old buildings. I hadn't seen cobbles like this in a city centre before and my thoughts immediately turned to the events in Paris in 1968, when students and young workers joined forces to strike, riot and take-part in teach-ins at the universities in order to plan a new, better society. Their most famous slogan was, 'under the cobblestones is the beach'. I could see how tempting it would be to loosen these stones from their sandy bed and use them as weapons, and I wondered if this demonstration would remain peaceful.

The demonstrators had come from all over Europe and the square was vibrantly bedecked with multi-coloured flags and banners in Spanish, Italian, German and French. As I looked up at the tall, typically Flemish buildings with second floor balconies, I saw a red CND beret on top of the six-foot-eight-inch Rip Bulkley from the Oxford Campaign Atom Direct Action group, looking every bit a true, revolutionary leader. Was he going to give a rousing speech urging us to tear down NATO with our bare hands? Disappointingly he didn't, and after an hour of aimless milling about some shouting erupted, people cheered, the chanting started, and we were off.

The plan was to march to the NATO headquarters to demand dialogue with East Europe instead of nuclear escalation. I wore my trusty Doc Martens, jeans and donkey jacket. Sam sported black jeans, suede shoes, a tailored coat and a Palestinian scarf. Phil and Sarian had, inexplicably, disappeared, so we were on our own. After about forty minutes, we were out of the main built-up area and suddenly we were pushing up against the people immediately in front of us. The heavily-armed Belgian riot police had put large wooden barriers swathed in barbed wire across the road. The cops stood impassive, behind dark glasses and visored helmets, casually pointing sub-machine guns at us. Sam and I were among the large German contingent, who were getting angry as the crowd behind pushed into us, not knowing about the blockade ahead, so increasingly we were getting squashed up against the cops and the barbed wire.

Fizz! Bang! Fizz! Bang! Fizz! Bang!

Smoke and panic filled the acrid air swirling round us.

'They've bloody well started shooting,' said Sam.

They hadn't, thank god, but the German anarchists had started throwing firecrackers over our heads at the police, who seemed to be cradling their weapons with greater intensity. I had a sharp stabbing pain of fear in my guts; I wasn't good with violence. Sam was losing his rag and pushing forward into the barriers.

'They've got no right to stop us, let's just push these barriers over.'

'Can't you see the machine guns and water cannons, mate?' I countered nervously.

I grabbed Sam's arm and we wove out to the side of the crowd, which had spread out over some wasteland. I gradually managed to calm him down. We were sitting on the floor, smoking odd tasting Belgian fags, when a bronzed, middle-aged Spaniard stood up on a nearby rock. With his fist shaking, his marvellous hawk-like nose in profile and his dark hair swept back off his imperious face, he was shouting for all he was worth.

'We march on NATO now!'

Despite this fervent appeal, we didn't get any closer to our original destination. No one really wanted to get a kicking, or worse, from the goons with guns. I wonder now if he had been an *agent provocateur*.

After the demonstration, we went back to a university where we were to be fed and have the chance to attend meetings with activists from around Europe. I did manage to get some food, but I was too tired for meetings and found my way to our accommodation for the night. This was a marquee pitched in the yard of a community hall. Unfortunately, the yard was cobbled: less romantic as a bed than as revolutionary ammunition. It was cold, staggeringly uncomfortable and, to cap it all, a loud rock band was playing in the community hall. Phil and Sarian, it transpired, had missed the march in order to get together in a cheap hotel, where they stayed the night. Sam gave up the unequal struggle to sleep, and went off to join the party next door. I spent six hours of purgatory on the cobbles until I could stand it no more and went off in search of early-opening shops. We finally got back to Oxford late that night, cursing Gordon to hell and back.

Despite the disappointments of this trip, I had been inspired by seeing groups from all over Europe in the demonstration. The peace movement was growing fast across the continent and I believed that it could lead to a mass mobilisation of citizens on both sides of the Iron Curtain – a movement that governments couldn't ignore.

4

Gathering Greens

In the summer of 1981, on my quest to become a full-time revolutionary, I was perched amongst a load of camping gear in an old VW camper van as it bumped and wobbled across the rough grass. Small settlements dotted the valley in front of us. The most impressive were the majestic tipis of the Tally Valley tribe and their more prosaic collection of old buses and ex-ambulances. The blue and white circus marquee of the Tibetan Llamas stood tall and gleaming in the bright sun. The rest was a jumble of family frame-tents – more used to the Dordogne – tarpaulin-covered benders, two-man tents like mine in green and orange, vans, battered Land Rovers and even the odd caravan. Colourful flags flew, as best they could in the slight breeze, above most camps and occasional wisps of wood-smoke drifted in the hot summer haze.

I had arrived at the Ecology Party summer gathering, held on the site of the Glastonbury festival in Pilton in Somerset. We were to spend a week creating a mini-utopian community, exchanging knowledge and ideas and planning the growth of Green politics in the UK. This was very much a minority pursuit at the time, and most of the other folk at the gathering were middle-aged: old hippies (soon to be called New-Age travellers), renewable energy enthusiasts with their home-made windmills and solar showers, beekeepers, herbalists, conservationists, smallholders and political activists who had mostly been involved in non-party radical politics in the sixties and seventies. Those of us of student-age could have fitted comfortably into a Mini – so how come I was one of them?

At school I discovered that I had a real gift for Economics. It was my teacher in that subject, a clever, fat, sweaty and usually acerbic man who delighted in my progress and encouraged me to try for Oxford. He also encouraged the class to read the *Economist* magazine. So, one day in January 1979, I popped into the nearby town library after school. Down in the basement I found the periodicals room. I quickly found the *Economist* in the alphabetically sorted rack of publications, but my attention was taken by the magazine next to it: *The Ecologist*. It was advertising something called the *Blueprint for Survival*. This must have keyed into my worries about the possibility of nuclear war and environmental catastrophe, as I noted down the details, and later at home, sent away a subscription for the magazine and my free copy of the *Blueprint*.

I found the arguments for an ecologically sustainable society compelling, and I joined the Ecology Party in the summer of 1980. The Party had started to grow after the 1979 election when it had managed its first national TV broadcast. By getting into Oxford, I found myself in one of the country's Ecology Party strongholds. The city boasted at least a dozen committed activists, inspired by Jon and Jenny Carpenter.

Jon was bearded, and *did* wear sandals sometimes, but he was a sharp political thinker and a true English radical. He had run community newspapers, had rudimentary printing facilities in his house, and ran the political bookshop which I had cycled past on my way to the last exam. Jenny was a seasoned and effective community campaigner, and between them they brought huge energy, warmth and experience to the Party. Their house was very much an open house, and they took me under their wing. It was there that I first learned how to cook good vegetarian food as well as how to run a campaign.

They belonged to a van-share co-operative and it was with them, in the shared van, that I arrived at the summer gathering. We set up camp and then I changed into my old rugby shorts, a multi-coloured cheesecloth shirt, and – with my CND pendant round my neck – set off to the information tent to find out what was on offer. Under the awning of the fading canvas frame-tent sat an intense, skinny man with uncontrollable hair and thick black glasses, banging away on a portable typewriter. He looked up, offered me a crudely printed sheet of re-cycled green paper and said:

'Here you are, hot off the press. There's important info about firewood and fires, and a list of workshops and events.'

I found a place to sit in the shade of a marquee and pored over the closely-typed print. I was immediately drawn to a workshop on Non-Violent Direct Action, a talk by some women from Die Grünen (the new German Green Party), an open forum on 'Where next for the Ecology Party?' and a session on Steady-State Economics. This last one

25

was about to start, and I rushed over to the appropriate tent. It was the first opportunity that I had had, since the debacle of my attempt at Green Economics with my tutor at Oxford, to talk to other people interested in the issue, and I took copious notes in my cheap exercise book.

The irony of my disillusionment with Oxford University – and the subject that got me a place there – is that it was encouraged precisely by the extra reading I had done to prepare for the entrance exams. I had already begun to question the validity of the assumptions made by classical economic theory, and when I discovered J.K. Galbraith's books, *The Affluent Society* and *The New Industrial State*, I devoured his eloquent critique of the present system of capitalism – based, as it is, on ever-increasing consumption. This led me on to reading a wide range of more critical works.

The Oxford Economics curriculum was old-fashioned and had not been updated to take account of the failure of orthodox theories to solve the economic crises of the 1970s (high inflation and high unemployment at the same time) or to anticipate future problems. I was, however, inspired by a booklet published by the World Watch Institute as I was preparing for an extended essay to be completed over Easter 1981.

I worked diligently over the holidays writing a seventeen-page piece on early 'Green Economics'. I focused on the human cost of resource shortages in developing countries; the environmental costs of ever-expanding demand for natural resources; the inflationary drivers of economic growth based on natural resource use; and the ignored yet vital role of war spending (particularly the Vietnam War but also the Cold War) in creating the 1970s inflation crisis. I was proud of the work I'd done.

Back at college for the beginning of the summer term I was feeling upbeat. I was on my way to see Mrs Peters for our weekly session of Economics, together with my tutorial partner, Andy. Mrs Peters was an impressive woman in her early 60s with close-cropped grey hair and lively blue eyes. She was noted in the college for being in the Labour Party and one of the very few left-leaning academics of the old guard. Her flat was on the first floor of one of those three-storey red-brick Victorian houses that give North Oxford its identity. Built late in the nineteenth century to accommodate the first dons to be married and to live out of college, they stood resplendent in cherry-blossomed streets. They had leafy, secluded gardens, front rooms fit for entertaining and attic rooms for the servants. They spoke to me of solidity, seriousness, sherry and seed-cake. Mrs Paul's house had been converted into flats. We approached through the weedy backyard to the black cast-iron fire escape staircase to her study, overlooking the college grounds. I bounced up the iron stairs looking forward to my tutor's approval for the hard work I had done and a discussion of some of the new ideas I had come across.

We went in through the French windows to the book-lined study and sat on the William Morris floral-print chairs, which were worn on the arms and faded by sunlight. There was a deep quiet, punctuated by the distant ticking of a grandfather clock. It was Andy's turn to read out his essay, as mine would have already been marked by Mrs Peters. After we had discussed Andy's essay, there were twenty minutes left – great I thought, plenty of time to discuss mine. Mrs Peters pulled out my seventeen-page handwritten labour of love with the expression of someone who had trodden in dogshit in the college quad, poked me in the chest with it and said:

'Come back next week with some Economics.'

That was it. We said nothing and left. My legs felt weak as I descended the fire escape. The air seemed to have been sucked out of the atmosphere and the buildings felt like they were pressing down on me. I was crushed. I stumbled the 400 yards back to my room in silence, closed the curtains, lay on my bed and wept. This was the moment when I started to think seriously about leaving the university. The narrowness of focus and the otherworldly atmosphere of the university were beginning to feel absurd. Outside of Oxford, Bobby Sands and nine other IRA hunger strikers were starving themselves to death. Brixton had been engulfed in riots in April and, later in July, an arrest in Toxteth, Liverpool, sparked nine days of rioting. These riots spread to Moss Side, Manchester, followed by other towns and cities across England. In June, Israel bombed a nuclear reactor in Baghdad at about the same time that I was getting on my bike at my Gran's house to cycle down to my last exam and an uncertain future.

Three months later I was at a gathering in the Somerset countryside with people who were aware of the threats to our world and who wanted to do something about them. I had been mostly attracted to the overtly political meetings at the gathering, but on a more personal level, as I was already interested in – but ignorant about – gender politics, I decided to go to Keith Motherson's 'unlearning manhood' session. I was finding that the whole process of becoming an adult was being hampered by our society's difficulty in dealing well with emotions, especially for men. As I had attended an all-boys school and grown up in a masculine-dominated household, I had no experience to call upon when I was wrestling with my fears for the world and my place in it.

The initial session spawned daily meetings of men who wanted to explore their responses to feminism, stereotypes of manliness and different sexualities. I found that I was instinctively pro-feminist. Perhaps there wasn't enough room in my small family for three alpha males and inevitably I had to take a less overtly masculine role than my Dad and older brother.

It was mind-blowing to have the evils of patriarchy, and the effects of the gender conditioning that we have all experienced, put to me by another man. It was uncomfortable to have some of my taken-for-granted assumptions challenged. However, it was the emphasis on the positives for men of embracing feminism that made the biggest impact on me. For example, the importance of being able, as a man, to embrace emotions, gentleness and caring. The third session explored being gay. I found that my feelings about physical intimacy between men had been very influenced by my traditional upbringing: the idea of homosexuality was repellent, but best dealt with by pretending it didn't happen. It's hard to believe now, but nobody in my world thought Elton John or Freddie Mercury were gay (or 'poofs', as we would have said at the time) and we didn't get the clue of Freddie's band being called Queen. My all-boys school was profoundly ignorant about sex and sexuality in all its manifestations.

As I sat on the floor of a tent, deep in the Somerset countryside with a bunch of truly gentle men, I soon realised that I didn't have much invested in hanging on to these traditional views. We explored simple physical contact, and I found the courage to hold hands with gay, bisexual and straight men in this supportive group. It was like running into the freezing English sea. I just had to do it, without thinking too much. I took a deep breath and held out my hand, which was firmly, but gently, grasped by my neighbour, a bearded red-headed man in his forties. The world didn't end, nor did I experience a frisson of sexual desire, but I did feel the high that comes from breaking a taboo, and several of us grinned wildly as a result. This powerful experience almost instantly dissolved any fears I had about homosexuality.

The lack of knowledge and understanding of how to think and talk about emotions in the masculine-dominated world I grew up in was a factor in me taking extreme decisions. At eighteen years of age, there had been no outlet for expressing my fears, anger and confusion at the adult world I saw before me. During the last few weeks of the lower-sixth summer term I had been starting to get frustrated with school – it had all begun to feel a bit hollow. This wasn't helped by the extra year I spent there, due to a year in France as a fifteen-year-old.

I had asked my form teacher and rugby coach, Mr Knight, for a chat. We walked slowly around the playground during a mutual free period and I tried to explain my worries:

'I'm just feeling fed up with things. I know I can pass exams, but what does it really mean?'

'You do know you came top in Economics, don't you?' replied Mr Knight.

'Yeah, I heard yesterday – I'm pleased of course. But it all feels a bit empty.'

'You're probably just a bit tired.'

'I've always tried hard at school and I've really wanted to please my Mum and Dad and the teachers, but now I feel like I should have a reason for myself, and I can't find one. I don't know what I want to do with my life,' I said.

Mr Knight, stopped and put a hand on my arm and said:

'Next year you're going to be Head Boy, take your Oxford entrance exams and I'm going to put you forward for a county rugby trial. Enjoy the summer and come back ready for all those challenges.'

'I know I should be excited… but at the moment I just feel empty about it,' I said.

'Don't worry son, you'll be fine,' said Mr Knight, as we went our separate ways.

It's not unusual for people in their late teens and early twenties to look at the future that they see mapped out for them and recoil in horror at the restrictions and responsibilities that this implies.

On sunny afternoons, I would gaze longingly out of the classroom windows as Mr Grant droned on about the Diet of Worms. I didn't want to spend my adult life cooped up in an office on precious English summer days. Who doesn't have these kinds of thoughts at this age? For me, though, they were getting tangled up with my more unusual political awakening, intellectual development and emotional struggle over my changing understanding of the world and what my place in it should be.

I became more bolshie at school and at home as I sought to be treated more as an adult. Despite achieving what they had always wanted, the development of my liberal, political and economic ideas inevitably led me to conflict with my parents, who were *conservative* and Conservative. I had started studying politics in November 1978, just in time for the Winter of Discontent. Strikes, power-cuts, rubbish in the streets, the dead lying unburied and the Army's Green Goddess fire-engines were the subject of daily conversation at the tea-table – at six o'clock sharp we had bread, cheese, jam and a piece of cake for our evening meal. Dad and Mum would fulminate against the over-mighty trade unions, their Communist leaders and the craven Labour government.

'They're a disgrace – bringing the country to its knees. You know that the unions use bully-boy tactics to intimidate ordinary workers at their mass meetings, don't you?' said Mum.

'Yes, the leaders aren't interested in their members, they want to have a revolution – and in any case, we simply can't afford to keep paying higher wages to the public sector, it's just fuelling inflation, which is making life hard for all of us,' added Dad.

'Well maybe a revolution would be a good thing,' I said with teenage bravado.

'Don't talk such tommyrot,' Mum said loudly, 'what do you know about the world anyway, you're still a child.'

This accusation cut to the heart of my fragile seventeen-year-old ego, and I upped the ante. 'It's all right for you, you're comfortably off, by world standard's you've got rich supporting the racist British Empire in Africa and working for a giant chemical corporation whilst millions of babies are dying of starvation.'

'How dare you. We've worked hard for everything we've got. We've not had anything given to us on a plate. We're certainly not racist; if you'd lived in Africa, you'd know that a lot of the problems are down to the Africans themselves.' Dad raised his voice.

'But that's racist in itself!', I said hotly, risking a clip round the ear.

'You're pushing it too far now – I'm not going to be talked to like that in my own house,' said Dad as he marched off to smoke his pipe and do the *Telegraph* crossword.

'People are too selfish for communism to work, and anyway it's you I'm worried about, not the whole world,' said Mum, as I chomped on the remains of my fruit cake. 'You've got to get a good job if you want to get a house and look after a family – my god, we worked so hard to get all this – I suppose you think it's been easy for us?' I scowled and got up from the table and went to stew in my own juice upstairs, listening to Radio Caroline. I was as upset as my parents after these kinds of rows – I hated conflict, and more than anything I still craved their approval.

So, I was eager to learn about new ways of approaching personal as well as political relationships, which started for me in Keith Motherson's sessions at the Ecology Party gathering. Up till then I had not realised how important sexism was as an issue in radical politics. A few older men argued that combating sexism was a diversion from campaigning for an ecologically healthy society. Keith explained how the destruction of the natural world was intimately connected to male dominance and patriarchal values. These values conflated women with nature and despised both. We didn't just talk and hug, but volunteered to help in the crèche and agreed to monitor and challenge overt sexism in meetings and discussions at the gathering from other men. Trying to live out our ideals rather than just preach about them was central to the Green movement.

Earlier in the year, back in Oxford, I had been busy campaigning in a variety of local elections. And I got my first taste of canvassing the Great British Public. I knocked on a door in East Oxford and it was opened by a woman in her forties.

'Oh, hi there, I'm canvassing for the Ecology Party. Have you considered voting for our excellent candidate Phil Foggitt in the council election?'

'Oh, bless you. I think you seem lovely people with good intentions. But my husband says you are living in cloud cuckoo land,' she laughed.

31

'Well, cloud cuckoo land is a lot nicer than here and now,' I shouted over my shoulder as I walked away.

The summer gathering had been a temporary utopian experiment, and indeed it was like living in cloud cuckoo land for seven days. I experienced an uplifting sense of community and left at the end of the week buzzing with ideas and optimism for the future.

I was rudely jolted back to earth when I returned to England in mid-September after two weeks camping in the Black Forest with my girlfriend Clare, who had spent the summer as an *au pair* in Cologne. She went back to college and I went back home to Chelmsford for a few days. Dad cajoled me into visiting the Careers Service to get advice on different university courses that I could apply to for the following autumn, if I was determined not to return to Oxford. The County Careers Service was housed in a bleak concrete municipal building on the opposite side of Chelmsford to our house. Dad drove me there in silence.

There was no private room for the chief careers officer, only a messy desk in the middle of a large open-plan area. Several harassed-looking staff were buzzing around with piles of paper. It was mid-September and the clearing process for last-minute university entries was in full swing.

We met Mr Fairfax and I said: 'Hello, I'm Chris Savory.'

Before we could sit down, he jabbed a finger angrily towards my chest, his nostrils flaring, his face flushed: 'Every day of the week I've scores of young people coming to see me who would give their right arm for what you've given up, and now you come here asking for my help. I haven't got the time for this.'

So, I was only acceptable as a human if I toed the line and didn't think for myself. I'll show you, you bastards, I thought. I *will* find a way to be authentic *and* change the bloody world into the bargain.

5
Class Struggle

I was no stranger to being on the receiving end of other people's anger for seemingly no reason at all, and the roots of my wider political awakening lay in my childhood experiences of Chelmsford, where we had moved when I was five. Our house was next to the park, on the outskirts of the biggest council estate in the town. One Sunday morning Pete and I were on the swings in the playground when a group of older lads from the estate gathered round us. The leader told us that he had dropped his watch in the river and that he wanted us to find it for him. After a few threats we went down to the river and started to paddle around looking down into the water for the watch. The lads had gathered on the concrete jetty and were giving advice, jeering and splashing us. Then, suddenly, as I was bending down, a half brick brushed past my head and went on to hit Pete on his hip. The gang then sauntered off.

We ran up the hill home and found Dad in our front garden tending his roses, bare-chested in his old African khaki shorts. We told him tearfully what had happened, and he immediately jumped over our low brick wall and ran off down to the park. Dad was six-foot-two, fourteen stone and fit and strong. Pete and I followed at a safe distance and watched Dad approach the bullies. Having discovered the boy who had thrown the brick, he proceeded to cuff him round the ears and kick his backside in full view of all his mates. This didn't stop future incidents with other groups of older children, however. Pete and I continued to be the targets of constant, low-level bullying and the occasional more serious attacks over the next seven or eight years.

I started at the King's Road Junior School in September 1968. By today's standards, it was huge, with a four-class entry of around 150 children each year – the tail end of the post-war baby boom. The school was built in the 1920s to serve the new council housing estate. About four-fifths of the pupils lived on the estate while the rest of us lived in the adjacent roads to the south and east.

In the A-stream class of fifty pupils, only about ten lived on the estate. Only two or three in the B-stream didn't live on the estate, and the C and D-streams were 100% estate kids.

Chelmsford was a thriving industrial town in the 1960s, as well as being the administrative centre for Essex, so there was plenty of work. However, most of the poorest and most dysfunctional families in the town lived on the estate. It was impossible not to notice those children who came into school stinking, those who had to be kitted out from the lost property box because their clothes were too ragged or inappropriate, and those who keeled over in assembly from lack of food.

I experienced resentment all the time from older children on the estate who bullied and frightened me most days of the week on the journey to and from school, year after year. It wasn't only the children who were resentful. In my third year at Junior School, our year group had expanded so much that a dozen of us (the highest achievers) were put up a year, in order to even-up both classes to around fifty children each. We, of course, were all children of families who lived away from the estate. Seven of us were boys, and naturally enough, we would hang around together at break times. One day in the summer term, we had finished our school dinner and left the canteen, which was away from the main school site next to the playing field. We were dawdling back to the playground, kicking a tennis ball around, having fun. The perpetually grumpy figure of Mr Stephens loomed into sight and made a beeline towards us. He was the D-stream teacher in our year group, a man in his late fifties with shiny thinning hair and a fraying dark green cardigan with leather buttons.

'What are you lot up to?'

'Nothing, Sir, just on our way back to the playground,' I said.

'You're going to be late if you're not careful.'

Alan Owers looked at his new wristwatch: 'It's only ten to one, Mr Stephens, we've got ten minutes.'

'Don't be cheeky boy. I'm sick of the lot of you. You're just are a bunch of spoilt brats who've got far too high an opinion of yourselves. Now give me that ball and get out of my sight.'

This may sound trivial, but it cut me deeply. It was so patently unfair, and I was a good boy who worked extremely hard to follow

34

the rules in order to make sure I was never told off. I expected authority figures to be pleased with me.

I enjoyed Cubs and then Scouts, which were also based on the estate, and I carried on as a Scout after passing the eleven-plus and going to the Grammar School. Once, when I was thirteen, I was leaving the church hall at the end of the regular Thursday evening session, when Bradley Davies, a big lad who was two years older than me, barred the way.

'Where do you think you're going?'

'Just leaving to get my bike and go home.'

'Little prick' – he spat out the words as he swung round and punched me in the face.

I told the Scout leader, Tony Hewitt, but he did nothing. Two years later he told me that he would never make me a patrol leader because Grammar School boys got too much already.

So, before I even knew that the word sociology existed, I was developing a keen understanding of social class. I felt the anger, jealousy, resentment – hatred even – of a community that knew that the odds were stacked against them. I was scarred by this resentment, feeling it viscerally. It felt so unfair. I was just being me. I didn't feel so lucky or privileged or special. I certainly didn't think I had done anything to deserve the barbs from the adults. As I grew up, it burned deep and I started to feel guilty and think that maybe they were right to resent me and my kind. The world was clearly set up to favour some and to make life hard for others, based solely on who their parents were. If these early experiences of inequality and its effects gave me a solid base for understanding social class, then my summer job between school and university as a dustbin man was a masterclass. I learned so much from those eight weeks on the bins. Getting up at 5 am to gulp a quick bowl of cereal, making sandwiches and cycling the four miles to the yard in time for a 6:15 am start, was a shock to the system. I realised how tough this would be in the winter when it was dark and cold. On the first day there were two of us new relief workers. There was no round for us to join, so we had to clean the yard, including the toilets. The rest of the week was spent on 'specials'. The first job was to clean up a recently vacated traveller's camp. That involved a lot of actual shit as well as casually-strewn rubbish, half-hidden in the long grass and bushes.

Day three was spent cleaning up huge mounds of rubble from the back garden of an empty council house.

Later, as I became more politically engaged and embraced non-violence as a way of life, I used Gandhi's insistence, that everybody should clean up their own mess, as a guiding principle in my own life – in no small part influenced by my time as a dustman. I still firmly believe that in order to be respected by others, and to be equal members of society, you should be prepared to clean up your own mess, and not expect others to do it for you. This applies right across the board, from travellers and council house tenants to the rich, who expect poor people to change their baby's nappies, pick up their dog's shit and clean for them at home and at work. Of course, the concept of 'dealing with your own mess' is much wider than literally dealing with waste, but I think it's a great place to start. From the bottom up, as it were. If everyone took on that responsibility, how much harder it would be to look down on other people, and how well self-importance is pricked when you get down to work with a scourer and a toilet brush! Then we could move on to deal with the air pollution in our cities, the plastic in our seas and the nuclear waste no one knows where to store. We are a society that manifestly does not deal with its own mess!

During the summer of 1980 I also learnt that many people look down on you if you are doing a low-status job. As a dustman, you worked physically hard, dealt with maggot-infested bins and lived with the constant smell of decaying rubbish – and all for a relatively low wage. One day, I was on a rural round, just me and the driver. I was dropped at a bungalow in the middle of nowhere. There was no sign of the bin out front, so I started to go around the back. I froze on hearing the deepest, most frightening bark I'd ever heard. I really didn't want to come face-to-face with whatever was making that bowel-churning noise. I knew I was supposed to get the rubbish so I was reluctant to retreat, but my courage deserted me and I remained rooted to the spot in terror. Then, a cut-glass voice broke the spell.

'For goodness sake, he's not going to hurt you, you silly man.'

Over in the flower garden, a middle-aged woman in floral apron was delicately gathering flowers into her wooden trug. I was sure she didn't speak to her Great Dane with such contempt in her voice.

Since then, central government has squeezed council budgets, curtailed union rights and enforced the privatisation of basic services like refuse collection. This has made it much harder for workers to fight erosions to their pay and conditions. It is not unusual for refuse collection staff to be employed by a private company via an agency and to be paid the minimum wage. The sheer pace of the work is hugely demanding and, at least in some places, crews must now work all public holidays except Christmas Day. So, the workers, who stop the rest of us being submerged in our own waste, are paid a pittance for hard physical work, no perks and no pension scheme. At the same time, council housing has been sold off and the basic costs of running a home since 1980 have gone up way beyond inflation. Would going on strike back then have helped hold back this tide? It is very hard for people at the bottom of society to risk what they have in order to fight for a possible better future. I, however, on the verge of taking up my place at Oxford, decided I would no longer be able to study Economics as a purely abstract subject – a subject that ignored the everyday reality of people's lives. Those lives that were on the receiving end of policies built on nice clean graphs and mathematical models.

6
Greenham Common

Towards the end of my idyllic week at the Ecology Party summer gathering near Glastonbury, my friend Jenny from Oxford called out to me across the field:

'Come over here, Chris, we've got to give them a proper send-off.'

'They' turned out to be a group of about thirty women plus some men and children with banners, pushchairs, backpacks and flags. They were the 'Women for Life on Earth' peace walkers who had visited the gathering *en route* from South Wales to RAF Greenham Common in Berkshire. As they finally moved off in higgledy-piggledy fashion out of the farm gate and to the lane, we clapped, whistled, cheered and shouted encouragement and congratulations. Greenham, like Molesworth where I had gone for my first CND protest, was a site designated for the new American Cruise Missiles. It was, as yet, largely unknown.

This was to change after some of the women from the march decided to stay and set up a peace camp at the main gates of the base, in order to bear witness to the decision to site the new nuclear bombs there. These so-called 'smart weapons' were piloted by on-board computers to increase their accuracy. Along with the Pershing 2 missiles in Germany, they were an intrinsic part of the Reagan administration's plan for a first-strike policy, and thus a 'winnable' nuclear war.

My second connection to Greenham came about via a workshop on Non-Violent Direct Action at the summer gathering, which had in turn led to a conference at the Conway Hall in London on the day after the national CND demonstration in London in October 1981, where over 250,000 people had rallied in Hyde Park. There were around fifty attendees at the conference, including veterans of the Committee of 100 and other white-haired anarchists. There were only a very few young people. The mood quickly turned impatient. All of us, I think, felt frustrated at being part of the vast crowd which had come together the day before with such passion, but which had then melted away to nothing, probably making no impact at all on the government. We weren't going to be satisfied with just talking on this day. Someone suggested going to the nearby *Guardian* offices to protest about their lack of coverage of the Greenham Common Peace Camp. As far as I know, Greenham was the first peace camp in the UK outside a military base and it was to become an iconic part of both the peace and women's movements. At first, though, it was small and unknown. The *Guardian* was – and still is – the only consistently left-of-centre newspaper in Britain, but it wasn't far enough from the centre for many of us in the peace movement as it remained resolutely opposed to unilateral disarmament. So, we didn't have our views reflected anywhere in the national media, and this made the *Guardian* a suitable, if embarrassingly soft, target for our anger.

We straggled along the London pavements at about 4 pm. The newspaper offices were open, and we filed in. It was a spacious lobby with a reception desk staffed only by a couple of security guards as it was Sunday. We hadn't formulated a proper plan, so we milled around a bit while a small group of self-appointed leaders spoke to security. Then someone sat down on the floor and said that we should all sit down and block the foyer until a representative from the paper would speak to us. Great, I thought, this is it, direct action at last! In the end we sat on the floor for about an hour before a journalist agreed to talk to three of our number and hear our concerns. This felt like an important first step in getting my career in direct action off the ground. I had actually done something that I shouldn't have – out of principle! I had moved from passive protest to action.

Back in Oxford at Campaign Atom (the local CND group) we knew all about the camp and were close enough to give practical support. As usual I went to a regular Tuesday night meeting in late November. We mostly discussed the march that we were planning in December, in Oxford city centre, against cruise missiles. The last item on the agenda was an urgent request from the Greenham Peace Camp. Berkshire Council was trying hard to evict them. They had already forcibly removed one lot of tents, and some women had been served with injunctions to keep them away from the base. A second eviction was threatened imminently, and the camp was currently very vulnerable on weeknights, as it was sometimes unoccupied. The core of women who started the camp were not thinking in terms of living at the site for years, as some women eventually did. Instead, the camp was a focal point from which they would take their campaign against cruise missiles across the country, meaning that women were travelling great distances to speak at meetings. Weekends were well covered, as plenty of people were able to visit the camp on non-workdays, but the women were asking for volunteers to stay at the camp during the week, in order to hold the fort – to use an entirely inappropriate metaphor. Most of the members of Campaign Atom were middle-aged and in jobs and many had children to look after, preventing them from dropping everything at a moment's notice. That didn't apply to me, so off I went. I found a lift on Thursday that week from a woman who was going down to the camp with some food. I got my tent, sleeping bag and mat, camping stove and as many warm clothes as I could find, and stuffed them into my rucksack.

We drove in the usual heavy A34 traffic on a grey, blustery, late-November morning, arriving at the peace camp at lunchtime, carrying flasks of soup, bread and a sumptuous looking fruitcake. The base occupied a large area of heathland, and on arrival all I could see behind its fences were trees and scrub. In front of the gates and barbed wire-topped fencing was the Peace Camp's Portacabin, a couple of frame tents and a few smaller tents on the other side of the entrance road. The missiles weren't in the base yet, and as construction work had not yet begun in earnest, it was pretty quiet.

Helen John, one of the founders of the camp, was there, so I was able to introduce myself to her. She was delighted that someone had answered their appeal for help and filled me in on the details of the evictions and how the peace camp worked. It was the Women for Life on Earth peace camp, and women were running the show. Men were welcome as long as they respected this.

Although it would have made Robert Baden-Powell spin in his grave, it is true to say that my time in the Scouts had prepared me well for life in a peace camp. Not the knot-tying or church parades, but coping with cold, dirt and the lack of bathroom and kitchen facilities. It got dark soon after 4 pm and the cold got through to your bones, regardless of how many layers you were wearing. I had yet to discover the joys of thermal underwear, so I was still rather underdressed in my jeans, T-shirt, shirt, hand-knitted sweater, donkey jacket and woolly hat. I was keenly aware of how important a fire would be for the long evenings so, when I wasn't helping to greet visitors, I busied myself collecting firewood from the wide verge of scrub, trees and gorse bushes that surrounded the airbase.

The weekend passed quickly with a flurry of visitors and all the time-consuming tasks of fetching and carrying water, digging shit-pits, boiling water and washing up from mealtimes. On the following Tuesday, the last woman left the camp and for three days and nights I was left in charge, with only two young Irish lads for company. The older one had lush, wavy black hair, played the guitar and had something of the young Donovan about him. Neither gave much away about who they were, except that they were from Donegal and had been travelling for six months together. If the police, military or bailiffs had decided to move us on, I think the lads would have scarpered sharpish in order to avoid contact with the authorities, and I certainly couldn't have saved the camp on my own.

Luckily, we were mostly left alone. We had some crisp, cold days and intensely dark starry nights that you only get in the country, away from streetlights. The airbase formed an eerie backdrop to our messy squatters' camp. Places connected to war and weapons of mass destruction emanate a cold tangible sense of death – to me, at any rate. It was a blessing that we had a musician with us, and I spent several hours each night sitting round the fire listening to 'Donovan' playing and I joined in with the songs I knew. There we were, huddled round the fire, toasty fronts and freezing backs, just outside the gates of the airbase, being observed by equally cold sentries as they made their rounds inside the fence. Sparks flew up from the fire to join the fierce stars as I joined in with lustly melancholy to 'Mr Tambourine Man', that great poetic song of travel, imagination and wonder. Suddenly there was a burning sensation in my foot. I had got too close to the fire and melted the sole of my Dr Marten's boots. I leapt up, dancing an involuntary, curse-laden jig until I found water to slosh on to the melting plastic. The plastic soon set hard in the cold night air, giving me a personal souvenir of my time at Greenham Common.

After two weeks at the camp I got a ride back to Oxford so that I could have a bath and do some washing. I left my tent where it was and expected to return in a few days to continue my guard duties.

The weather intervened however, and after a night back at Gran's in Cowley, I woke to a complete white-out. The snow stayed for well over a week, and when I finally managed to cadge a lift back to Greenham, my tent had disappeared. Upset at losing a trusty friend and with nowhere to sleep, I got a lift back to Oxford.

Over the last five months I had experienced the pattern that my life would follow for the next five years: periods of intense activity, full of emotional highs and lows and excitement coupled with physical hardship, interspersed with periods of unstructured time. I didn't know what the immediate future might hold. I had visited three universities and been offered places for the following September on a range of different courses. I was trying to be sensible, but my desire to change the world was powerful. I was being torn apart by this inner battle. By leaving Oxford University after one year, I had gone against not only my family's hopes, but against the accepted wisdom of pretty much all of society. On the nights I sat up after my Gran had gone to bed, I was tortured with self-doubt, finding comfort in stuffing myself with whole packets of biscuits. Was I mad? – that is what my Economics tutor Mrs Peters had said to a friend of mine, when she heard I was leaving Oxford. Was I a well-intentioned but naïve young fool? Or was I right? Was the threat of nuclear Armageddon and/or ecological catastrophe so pressing that devoting one's life to stopping it was the only sane and sensible thing to do?

Perhaps I was a bit of all three.

7
To the Heart of the Beast?

During the months after I left university in June and began to experience life as a would-be, full-time activist, Mum and Dad came to stay for a weekend at Gran's. Dad and I were sitting in the sun-lounge on a warm Sunday morning in October. I had always felt safe here, amongst the geraniums and the gently-mouldering armchairs that were covered in multi-coloured crocheted blankets. As the Oxford air came to rest in this sun-lounge, it was warmed and infused with a sense of unhurried acceptance. It was hard to stay awake never mind get agitated, as we looked out at some improbably late-blooming roses and gnarly apple trees. This was just as well, as Dad and I were trying to communicate across the fault lines of generations, political differences and unspoken emotions.

'The roses are looking good for October,' I offered as an opening gambit.

'They could do with deadheading and a good prune in the winter – Grandad Ross never cut them back hard enough,' Dad replied.

'Biscuit?' I passed the battered floral tin across to Dad.

'It's always been good soil for roses though.'

'Peace Studies at Bradford will let me straight into the second year – I would have the fees and grant paid all the way through,' I started, on the real business of our talk.

'Wye College has always had a good reputation for Agriculture,' Dad said.

'Yeah – they did offer to take me, but I would have to catch up on a load of science. You know I gave up Chemistry A-level.'

'Did you know that I had to do a crash course in science when I switched from Classics to Forestry? I took to Botany and Geology straight away, but I failed Chemistry the first-time round.'

'Really, Dad? I didn't think you ever failed at anything, I thought you were perfect.'

Dad looked hard at me, his thin lips tightening. I looked away. We sat in silence, dunking our dry custard creams and slurping our coffee.

'There's a sandwich year on Peace Studies too – you get to work for a relevant campaigning organisation or charity, or maybe even the UN.' I got back to the matter in hand.

'It is hard to get into farming these days and there's no money in science,' Dad said.

'Middlesex Poly was a bit crappy, with horrible buildings, no atmosphere, and it wasn't very well organised. The course did seem good though – radical Town Planning – but again, I'd have to start in year one and find a way of paying for the final year.'

'Think you'll be all right up North? Bradford's a good deal rougher than Oxford.'

Dad finally acknowledged that I was choosing Peace Studies at Bradford University.

'I don't see why not,' I said, based on absolutely no knowledge at all.

'What are you going to do in the meantime?,' Dad asked.

'Peace stuff, conservation work, Ecology Party campaigning – I'm not sure exactly.'

'How do you fancy working in one of Rhone-Poulenc's factories in America for a few months?'

America? The land of Ronald Reagan, born-again Christians, Hollywood and its lies, Coca-Cola and rampant consumerism – everything I despised. Not to mention the mountains of nuclear warheads. Why would I want to go there – to the heart of the beast – and to work in an agrochemicals packaging factory? Me, an eco-activist - for goodness sake!

'It'll give you something to do, some money and the chance to travel over there and stop you loafing about for a year.'

I wanted to jump up and shout: I'm not planning to loaf about; I'm trying to save the world! But of course, I still felt like the little boy who was too scared to answer back, and so I said nothing and instead got up and walked to the end of the garden to fume.

Staring out across the city to those so-called dreaming spires of the university, I realised that the conversation that I had been dreading had gone much better than I expected. I thought Dad would be more obviously upset with me for leaving Oxford and choosing

44

Peace Studies. I was thrown off guard by his apparent acceptance of my choices and his offer to help me with a job in the States. I was still furious with him, though, for pushing me toward Oxford all my life, only to appear underwhelmed when 'all' I managed was to get into an ex-women's college to read PPE – a subject, he reminded me regularly, had frequently been the butt of jokes among his scientist pals.

In the end, the prospect of money, travel and adventure outweighed my fears of being contaminated by America and agrochemicals, and I gratefully – if ungraciously – accepted Dad's offer and prepared to become a factory worker in the Midwest.

I left England on New Year's Eve 1981, with my early twenty-first birthday present – a one-way ticket to Kansas City. Saint Joseph was a town sixty miles north, with deep snow everywhere.

The factory was a packaging plant, mostly for herbicides for the grain farmers of the Midwest and Great Plains. Stocks needed to be built up in the winter and so seasonal workers were taken on. I was soon to further the education I had received whilst working on the bins in Chelmsford, by experiencing production line labour.

For the first five or six weeks at St Joseph I kept a diary. My experience had a significant impact on my understanding of modern mass production. I thought a great deal about why people tolerate such boring lives and what stopped radical political change happening. Here are some excerpts:

Wednesday 6th. Talked to Greg – he's been working here for 7 years – he got married and now has a kid. That's why everyone puts up with it – cos everyone else does, and they don't know any alternative. That's the challenge, to find alternative ways to live. Then we get back to the old problem – what will induce people to do something new and different? I also thought about the amount of work that goes into the application of herbicides which we are making and packing. All that tin mining, oil finding, drilling and refining. Untold poor bastards sweating it out extracting so many minerals from the earth to make the containers, the machinery, the paints, the trucks, the trains, the ships, the concrete and the rubber and even the chemicals themselves. If all that work was added up it would seem to make sense to do that work on the land using biological methods. It means I wouldn't be on $56 a day and that the poor would be better off – but of course we need to learn to equally distribute land to those who can use it and want to use it. And there needs to be education.

Bill mentioned the fact that he thought there would be a nuclear war soon. The reaction was muted and I got the feeling that people are scared about it as well, but to be radical here soon gets you in jail, hospital or the loony bin. It's hard to see a grassroots political organisation working here in the United States. CND may succeed in England but I doubt it, because how can we hope to elect a government that would have the guts to defy the USA?

Thursday 7th. On the way to work Ed and I were talking and he said that all the money spent on defence would do much more good if it were spent on cancer research or something useful. Two mentions in two days on the nuclear issue – this shows how much it is on people's minds all over the world. I would indeed love to know what the people in Russia and China are thinking; I hope I will be able to find out one day. It does rather reinforce the urgency of the situation, after a while people will learn to live with a new level of terror until there is another significant increase. The same thing applies to the work – their outbursts of irritation or boredom – in particular on Friday. There seems to be a general consensus of opinion that they don't want to be stuck in the same hole all their lives – but then they have responsibilities, families, social pressure etc. which means they probably will be stuck in it.

Wednesday 13th. Today I spent all day capping small plastic containers of weed killer. It was tiring as it was almost non-stop work and also monotonous. You really get the feeling that you are an accessory to the machine, it is de-humanising – you have to become relentless, methodical, mechanical, predictable. You need people-machines or machine-people to live in a machine world. You can really see how the educational system fits so well with working life. Do what you're told when you're told, how you're told, and life is still regulated by bells – alarm clocks and bells telling you when to start, when to stop, it brutalises your soul. That's why I was always late to lessons in my last year at school – defying those bells becomes important. That's why university was hard; you had to make your own bells. They want you to internalise them, and then you can become the boss because you can make them ring for other people. So as a rebellion against those bells those of us who fight them became slobs. The challenge is, can I manage to be neither a slob nor a Pavlov's dog, but motivate myself to live a full life, positively?

Saturday 16th. The thought occurred to me on Thursday that after work I fell back into thoughtlessness. All the noise, the concentration, and the monotony: in order to survive you have to just plug into the routine, and bumble along. Meanwhile the net of oppression tightens and you never have *any control over your life. Thud, thud the factory rolls on, click, click the typewriter rattles, the bullets fly and the prison door bangs and the hungry cry and the cold shiver and the frightened tremble.*

Wednesday 20th. The majority of people here are trapped by psychological and social and educational barriers, the low paid are trapped by economic ones as well. They might want to change the economic situation and if things got hard enough, might do something politically, if they were given a helping hand to start. Most of the workers are male between the ages of 25 and 30. There are moans and groans about taxes, unemployment, inflation, violence, boredom. But no anger. There is some small anger against taxation and the police. There is a great deal of acquiescence and acceptance and apathy. Just like there is everywhere.

I don't really see a lot of hope for significant social change but I am resolved to carry on working things out in myself so I can really start to work effectively when I go back to England.

Sunday 31st. Some feelings about the excitement of industrialisation, seeing all the different products from all over the world that we use at the factory, if you're part of that chain, somehow the romantic image of modern society is possible to feel. Also it does feel good in a way to be able to say I'm working for a living, sweating some, getting paid at the end. Our society puts so much emphasis on work. I also get a strange feeling standing outside the plant, particularly at dawn. The beautiful sky on Thursday was the dawn coming up over industrial America. I can see why some people still have faith in the industrial process. There is something awe-inspiring about the whole scene. But then the grey afternoon wind bites at the rubble and deserted buildings all around – and the familiar strains of the Jam song lyrics come into my head: 'here amongst the shit the dirty linen and the holy Coca-Cola cans'. There is always the shit that no one ever clears up.

Tuesday 2nd February. Working on a production line is an abuse of the body and mind if I did it for long, I would be nervous wreck.

It was, of course, intensely lonely being cooped up in a bedsit with no friends and sub-zero temperatures outside. Luckily, I had been told about Servas by the brother of a school friend. It is an international travelling and hosting organisation that was set up after World War Two to promote peace and international understanding, through foreigners being welcomed into the homes of ordinary people. I managed to set up a weekend visit at the end of January with a

47

host in Kansas City and was able to talk properly with someone for the first time in six weeks, as well as to experience the joy of blue-berry pancakes. The most significant part of the visit was that my host had recently also given a bed to a participant in the World Peace March that went from San Francisco to New York. The marcher, whose name was Thomas and who was an American Buddhist, had left some information about the march and some contact details. I wrote to him giving my support and telling him something about what was going on in the UK peace movement. He wrote a lovely letter back, thanking me and encouraging me to join the march.

The second Servas host whom I stayed with, on several occasions, also had a profound influence on me. This was the Catholic Worker House in Kansas City. It was a hostel for homeless men and a peace centre with a good library, and the focus of local peace activity. Father Dick and Sister Barbara were inspirational people who fully embodied the Catholic Worker tradition that had started during the Great Depression. Their mission was to help people in great need, but also to challenge society to stop creating such need.

Shalom House was comprised of a communal front room with picture windows – from when the building had been a shop – a bunk room behind for eight men, a kitchen and bathroom downstairs, pri-vate quarters upstairs for the staff (where I slept on a sofa in the living room), and a small but very well-stocked peace library and resource centre.

The simple service on a Sunday morning, held in the commu-nal room downstairs, was not compulsory for the men, but several attended. One of the lay helpers, Dana, played guitar and led the sing-ing; Dick and Barbara led the prayers and we broke bread together. It always seemed to be sunny and the large windows allowed plenty of light and warmth into the room. The experience for me was spiritu-ally deep and humbling as I prayed with these homeless men whose lives had fallen apart, and who were now painstakingly trying to get them back on track. I particularly remember Mark, a beautiful young black man who had what we would now call mild learning difficul-ties. He was slow, but not stupid, gentle and kind but he needed help and support to be able to find suitable work and somewhere to live where he would have people around to keep an eye on him. Mark's mother couldn't afford to keep him at home any longer and he had ended up sleeping rough in the Midwest winter. I held hands with Mark as we said the Lord's Prayer. My heart was full of love for this gentle soul and my mind was full of anger that this was happening in the richest nation on earth. Shalom House showed me the truest form of Christianity that I had ever experienced. It was after this visit, and seeing people actually living out their ideals in a practical and inspiring way, that I wrote to my long-standing girlfriend Clare back in England, in all seriousness, if a little pretentiously, to explain that our lives were moving apart as I was now dedicating myself to a simple life in search of truth.

I made three weekend visits to Shalom House and then stayed a week at Easter. As a protest, Sister Barbara and her Benedictine order of nuns led the Stations of the Cross in the city centre on Good Friday. We went to various points around the city that were connected in some way to the arms trade or the military. This bland modern city of skyscrapers and glass-fronted office blocks was rife with arms manufacturers and military offshoots. President Eisenhower had been right to talk about 'the military-industrial complex' dominating American life. We sang the hymn 'Were You There?' outside these building and, as we processed with our cross, we were followed by a large number of police and men I assumed to be FBI agents, who continuously photographed and intimidated us.

During my second visit to Shalom House I met Richard Sauder. By then he had already staged some solo protests at military sites in Louisiana, where he had been working in a salt mine. He had served a short prison sentence and was being advised by his supporters in the local Catholic Church to rein in his illegal activities. He was disinclined to take their advice, and so had sought refuge at the Catholic Worker House here in Kansas once he had been released from jail. Richard was a few years older than me (mid-twenties) when we met, about my height at around six-foot-two, and strongly built after the rigours of the salt mine. He was square-jawed and big-featured, with intense green-grey eyes. In contrast to my hairy countenance and old work clothes, Richard was clean shaven and wore a brown three-piece suit, polished shoes and a conventional haircut, albeit with an extravagant fringe. When animated, the fringe would flop over his face, and Richard would sweep it back with alarming speed and energy.

49

*Fig. 3. Left to right: Bill, Mark, John, Richard Sauder,
Sister Barbara, Father Dick*

We hit it off immediately and became firm friends. I did not share Richard's deep faith, but we did share an inability to ignore, dissemble or pervert the fundamental Christian message. In the Sermon on the Mount, Jesus of Nazareth unequivocally preached a crystal-clear message of peace and forgiveness. I found the fact that Christian clergymen had blessed the atomic bombs that were dropped on Hiroshima and Nakasaki disturbing and mind-scrambling. Rather than forgive our enemies, we were preparing to blow them and the rest of humanity to kingdom come. When you can't block, ignore or rationalise away these thoughts, you find yourself in an extremely uncomfortable place where at some point action becomes a necessity for mental and emotional survival. In April 1982, we were experiencing the height of President Reagan's 'Christian' crusade against atheist Communism. At the same time, Reagan and his administration were fighting increasingly dirty proxy-wars in Central and South America and the Caribbean. Like me, Richard found that he simply had to protest.

The mid-west had around one thousand inter-continental ballistic missiles (ICBMs), sited well away from centres of population and dotted around to avoid block-targeting by Soviet missiles. These Minutemen missiles, named after the civilian militia in the American War of Independence, each carried warheads capable of destroying whole cities and all the people in them. They were on alert 24/7 and were manned by operators whose whole working life was spent practicing and waiting for the signal to participate in the destruction of human civilisation and possibly human life itself. (450 updated versions of these ICBMs were still operational in 2018.)

Richard borrowed a car and we drove out together into the empty plains of Kansas to look for missile silos. After the miles of regulation flat fields, straight roads and the occasional farmstead and gas station, the high fence and squat concrete buildings inside were hard to miss. We parked up outside to recce the place. Almost immediately a military jeep roared up and braked unnecessarily sharply next to us. As the dust cleared, we saw the reflector shades, crew cut and sub-machine gun of a military policeman.

'Can I help you boys?'

'Yes sir, we seem to have missed our turning for Pinesville, and we're not sure of the best way back,' said Richard, full of exaggerated politeness.

'Turn around, first left, then right at the crossroads. There's no need to hang around here, so off you go.'

'Okay officer, you have a nice day now.'

I said nothing but smiled sweetly for the camera that had been taking multiple pictures of us from the jeep. We turned around and drove back in a contemplative silence to Kansas City. Ten days later, after I had left for Pittsburgh and the World Peace March, a reporter from the Catholic Worker newspaper drove my friend back to the silo and took photographs as Richard climbed over the fence in his brown suit and knelt to pray, brandishing a large crucifix. There was no damage to property, no harm to people – just a man praying. Richard was arrested and later tried in court. The judge thought that an appropriate response to this act of non-violent piety was to send Richard to prison for three years. How much was I prepared to risk for my beliefs? Richard, with his altogether more spiritual way of operating, had upped the ante.

I could have worked for six months at the factory, but the tedium of the work and the lure of the World Peace March led me to give up after three. I was there just long enough to receive a surprise visit from my Dad, who had been out on the West Coast for business and had stopped over on his way back to see me. I will never forget the hug we had at Kansas City airport. We had never hugged properly before as adults, and despite the gulf that had opened up between us politically, it was a rare display of unconditional love that helped restore our relationship.

8
The World Peace March

Father Dick and Sister Barbara drove me to the station in their battered mustard-coloured Datsun. I was really sorry to say goodbye to two of the finest people you could hope to meet, but I was too young and restless to settle down in one place.

I climbed the steep steps of the train with my heavy pack on my back, ducking into the compartment. I looked again nervously at my flyer about the World Peace March, detailing the dates and places they would visit in the coming months. I hoped there hadn't been a change of plan, as this was 1982 and long before mobile phones and the internet – I was relying on this piece of paper.

I arrived in Pittsburgh late in the afternoon and found a bus to take me out to the far suburbs where the march was meant to be stopping for the night. So far so good, but I was tired and anxious. As I struggled off the bus and onto a nondescript and semi-deserted urban street, I wondered if this had been a good idea after all. There were boarded-up shops, graffiti and litter, along with a chilly wind. I looked again at my now tatty and forlorn piece of paper. Scanning desperately for a street sign, I finally saw an address above a shop. I wasn't on the road I wanted to be on. As I hesitated outside the heavily-barred liquor store, I glanced across the road and saw a woman of about thirty-five with very long reddish hair, wearing jeans and a multicoloured sweater – one of us, I thought.

I waved as I shouted, 'Excuse me,' in my British accent.

She smiled as I crossed towards her.

'Hi, I know this may sound ridiculous but I'm looking for a peace march led by some Japanese Buddhist monks who are meant to be arriving here somewhere; you haven't seen them by any chance have you?'

The woman laughed out loud.

'I'm Mary-Jane and I'm helping organise the peace march. We're staying a couple of blocks away. I'm on my way back now, so I can take you there.'

As we walked, I poured out my story, garrulous from the relief of rescue. We arrived at a community centre, went into the main hall, and there they were. Mary-Jane found Thomas, who I had corresponded with, and he beamed and hugged me like a long-lost brother. Still stunned, I was taken to the leader, the Rev. Yoshida, and was officially welcomed to the World Peace March. Over the next eight weeks I would get to know my fellow marchers well. My first impressions were a blur of introductions and anxiety. For six months or more I had been reading Buddhist literature, mostly western-oriented and Tibetan or Zen-influenced, and I didn't know anything about the Nichiren tradition that this group had emerged from. I was, though, hoping to find spiritual inspiration in addition to making a contribution to the peace movement.

The Buddhists were six Nipponzan Myōhōji monks, all Japanese except for Shantha, the lovely smiling Sri Lankan, one Nipponzan Myōhōji nun, a Japanese Zen monk who was more or less ostracized by the Nipponzan Myōhōji, a translator, three Japanese wannabe monks, as well as Thomas and Brian, two American devotees.

There was also a young, long-haired pro-Western Japanese guy, who found himself on the wrong side of the monk's anti-Western views and found refuge in Mary-Jane's arms and van, as she drove ahead each day to organise the night's stopover. The luggage was carried by Bob-the-bus-driver, a proper hippy who was using his own converted bus, had a lank ponytail and played Country Joe and the Fish on his cassette player. The only Westerner who spoke Japanese was a clean-cut, ex-navy diver, Gary, who had lived in Japan after he left the service, diving and fishing. Matt and Juli, whom I became close to, were social activists and socialists from Columbus Ohio, in their thirties. Ellen and Paul were also from Ohio, brother and sister Christian peace activists, and they were accompanied by Ellen's friend, Doris. A couple of long-haired surfer dudes from California, Bruce and Jeff, had made it all the way so far and were much tougher than they looked. Jeff was a big Monty Python fan, so we shared a lot of silliness and laughs. Larry and Michael were both Christian men in their early forties who had joined the march as it passed through their hometowns in the Midwest. Paul Owns-a-Sabre was a Lakota Sioux warrior. Jo, a devout German Christian, and Beate, a German peace activist, were the other Europeans – I was number thirty.

I carried the banner on my first day on the march as we walked into downtown Pittsburgh and the local paper took a picture and printed it the next day. There I was, proudly at the front of the march, wearing my Casey Jones striped workman's dungarees and bandanna, sporting a bushy beard and a broad smile. This is what I wanted to be doing. This seemed so important, so worthwhile. Now was the opportunity to change society for the better, and here I was with a bunch of people who wanted to do just that.

A few days later, I discovered that the monks and the devoted Buddhists fasted each Monday, every week. I don't do well missing meals and, to be honest, I err on the side of gluttony. However, this was my first Monday and only my fourth day with the monks, so I thought I would try to fit in. So, I fasted, drinking only water, and walked for fifteen miles. We arrived in downtown Johnstown Pennsylvania, a town which boasted a very active Peace and Justice group whose members were to put us up for the night. Matt and I went home with Stan Davidson, one of the coordinators of the group. We drove a few miles to his home in the woods and went inside to be greeted by the smell of a slow-cooked stew. It would smell good any time, but after a day fasting and walking it smelt heavenly. Oh, how I wish I could have eaten some, but as Matt and I were fasting, we explained to Stan and apologised for not sharing his food.

After the non-meal, we relaxed and chatted. Stan put on some Crosby Stills Nash & Young and got out a massive bag of home-grown grass and rolled a stonking great spliff. I smoked my share of this and the next.

I started to feel dizzy and lightheaded, getting that feeling of dis-association of mind and body, as I appeared to be floating above myself whilst slumping in Stan's big green leather armchair. I didn't say much but sat grinning like the idiot I was. We were tired from the walk and the long day, and went up to bed, which turned out to be a mattress on the floor. Matt fell into a deep sleep. The whirling in my head kept me awake, but after an uncomfortable hour I slept.

In the middle of the night, I woke from a dream in a cold sweat. Except I didn't realise it was a dream. How could I have been so stupid and let the FBI trick me like this? They had set a honey-trap, got us to take drugs, recorded it all on a secret film, and any time now would come crashing into the house, arrest us and kick me out

Fig. 4. Jo, left, and Gary, carrying the banner. Rev. Yoshida is behind Jo on the right

of the country in disgrace. What a fool I'd been, and after only a few days on the march. How ashamed I would be when the monks found out what had happened. I felt shaky and sick with worry. I also felt hungrier than I can ever remember feeling – the 'munchies' from smoking dope – multiplied many times over by the fasting and the walking. I crept downstairs, still paranoid, still expecting a heavy knock on the door. In the kitchen I couldn't find the meal I had turned down earlier, which I had hoped had been left out on the stove. I couldn't find a fridge in the dark and the only food I could lay my hands on was a jar of peanut butter, which I crammed into my mouth with my fingers. It wasn't enough but it helped, and miserably I went back to bed, sleeping fitfully and full of anxiety until the dawn.

I resolved never, but *never*, to fast again.

We spent three weeks walking through Pennsylvania as April turned into May. We were warmly welcomed by a huge variety of church groups including Methodists, Quakers and the Salvation

Army, who put a few of us up for two nights in a homeless shelter. I had my twenty-first birthday in the historic town of Lancaster, and I sloped off at lunchtime and bought some shorts and a vest top as a present to myself, as the weather was warming up. May is a great month to have a birthday, and Lilac usually blooms in time for mine. It was in full flower in Pennsylvania that day and I picked a white one and a purple one and stuck them in my headband, savouring the sweet scent in the sunshine. I was now twenty-one, a proper adult. What was the future going to hold for me?

The Rev. Yoshida, our leader, was from Nagasaki, but he had been away from home as a teenage monk when the atom bomb had been dropped on his city. However, he lost most of his family and friends. Nearly every evening during our three weeks in Pennsylvania, we held a meeting for local people to encourage them to support the work of the UN. Yoshida-shoni would give a speech in Japanese that was translated, and then the film was shown about the bombing of Nagasaki. The grainy black-and-white film showed the shadows on the pavement that, moments before, had been flesh-and-blood human beings. People like you and me, people who shared food and love, people with hopes and dreams who were capable of generosity and meanness, kindness and hostility – all now gone, literally in a flash, to dust. The Rev. Yoshida talked about his city reduced to rubble and what it was like to see the aftermath and then to witness the next generation deformed at birth or dying prematurely of cancer. I saw that film and heard that speech more than thirty times before the end of the march. Every night it would sting me afresh, like a wound that never quite healed.

It's not as if the consequences of using science and technology, wealth, modern bureaucracy and communications in the twentieth century to unleash unprecedented aggression and hatred were secret. By the late 1970s we knew about the trenches of the Great War, the Nazi Holocaust, Japanese atrocities in South East Asia, Stalin's mass killings, the bombing of Dresden, Hiroshima and Nagasaki, the Mai Lai massacre and the carpet bombing and spraying of Agent Orange in Cambodia and Vietnam. At thirteen I had done a school project on Gallipoli and read first-hand accounts of the terrible war there. By fifteen I knew Wilfred Owen's poems. Every day at secondary school I saw a reproduction of Picasso's 'Guernica' hanging in the school corridor. I had read about the Nazis and seen the photos from the death camps. By nineteen I had read *Slaughterhouse 5* and Solzhenitsyn and seen *Apocalypse Now*.

However, most people alive in 1982 had not been directly affected by these events, and most people chose not to think too much about them. It's hard to keep faith in humanity, politicians and generals or even God when the scale of slaughter in the recent past is dwelt on. In the UK and America, there is a considerable degree of anti-Japanese sentiment, partly out of general racism, but made potent by the terrible cruelty experienced by Allied soldiers who were captured by the Japanese in Word War Two. I had been exposed to plenty of this feeling growing up, but listening night after night to this dignified Japanese man showing us how his city had been destroyed, and asking us to stop it ever happening again, made a powerful case for our common humanity to prevail over nationalism.

Knowing what people had done to each other over the last seventy years or so, and knowing that nuclear weapons had been used, why would anyone believe that the vast stockpiling of ever more powerful and sophisticated weapons was the best way to ensure that they were never used again? I was now devoting my life to working for disarmament and peace because I couldn't bear the fact that we were using our vast wealth, resources and some of the cleverest people on the planet, to invent, manufacture and deploy weapons that had the destructive power of thousands of Hiroshimas and Nagasakis. I had to do something. I had to go out in public and say: *No more Hiroshimas!* We must be better than this. We must find better ways of living together and resolving conflicts.

Due to being British and therefore something of rarity in the US, I was often asked to talk at these meetings about what was happening in my country. This gave me a role in the group that I relished as this direct communication with foreigners was empowering – bypassing, as it did, the partisan news media.

The World Peace March arrived in Washington DC on a hot sunny day in late May. Our first stop was the Pentagon – the nerve centre of the free world, or the heart of the beast. Take your pick. There's not much I can write about what was going on in that largely underground town, the blandness of the outside giving no hint of its inner workings.

Figs. 5a & 5b. Top: Three Mile island. Bottom: The Pentagon, with me in shorts holding the banner

Thirty thousand people worked there, we were told, and there was an entire shopping mall at the centre. Everything was top secret. What we did know, however, was that somewhere behind the outer concrete, clever, well-groomed, well-paid Americans were devising and preparing a nuclear first-strike policy which would mean the end of the previous policy of mutually assured destruction (MAD).

As we chanted outside in the sunshine, I could really sense the power and intensity of the monks' faith. I joined in, fully focussed, feeling the urgency of our task and hoping we could channel some of this 'peace force' into the hearts of the workers coming out for their lunch.

The monks, the would-be monks and their acolytes went to stay in the order's temple in a rich suburb of Washington, in Maryland. They would spend three days fasting, praying and then purging: torturing themselves in the lavish surroundings of solid gold Buddhas and heavy oak doors. Suffice to say that this bout of Japanese self-flagellation was not my cup of green tea, and I didn't ask to be included.

So, the unwashed and unfaithful stayed in a church in the poor black inner-city for three days, without a formal programme of activities. We were accepted by the local community, who saw our ragged appearance and opposition to 'the Man', rather than our white faces. Some of the more experienced campaigners realised that feeding thirty or so peace marchers would cost the church money it could better spend on its own people. So, it was decided that we would find our own food. Led by Jo from Germany – a devout Christian who had experienced real hunger as a child during the 1940s – along with Matt and Juli – the socialists from Ohio – a small team of us went out after dark, 'dumpstering'. We split into pairs and I went with the indefatigable Jo. We walked nonchalantly past a small row of takeaways and shops, then ducked round to find a back alley with access to the rear entrances. At the first, a Chinese restaurant, I held the torch as Jo crept in and opened the first bin. The putrid smell put off even the most determined scavenger. Our first success was a pizza place, in which the second bin revealed a batch of boxes with perfectly good looking pizzas. A quick sniff round gained my approval and four pizzas went into our bag. The grocery store next-door-but-one provided some healthy accompaniment with lettuce, tomatoes and peppers that were past their sell-by date. We were just fishing these out of the bin when an angry shopkeeper emerged.

'Get the hell out of my garbage!'

Any further comments were stopped in their tracks by his jaw dropping as he saw that his trash pilferer was a sprightly fifty-year-old white woman, who responded with: 'God bless you, sir.'

Back at the church, we pooled our 'loot'. Our pizza was the most appreciated, but we all dined in style on sandwiches, cakes, fruit, spaghetti and cheese. We carried on like this each day, and lived well on trash from the world's most wasteful society.

As we left Washington, we were now close to one hundred strong, as college students and workers taking vacations joined us for the final two weeks or so. Those of us who had been walking for some time were buoyed up by the new blood, able to pass on hard-won knowledge about the ways of the monks and dealing with blisters. Early on, I had taken a day in the luggage bus to rest my feet, and certainly felt the disdain, not from the monks themselves but their closest devotees. The monks, who had walked over most of the continents of the world, were always ready to help with dressing your blisters. Ex-professional baseball player Matsunanga-shoni would also regularly dispense muscular massages.

These extraordinary men and women had devoted their lives to the cause of peace. Some of them had already walked thousands of miles in places such as the Soviet Union and parts of Africa before crossing the whole North American continent. They really were *world* peace marchers, and their devotion to the cause was a massive inspiration.

As we made our way along the verges of the United States of America, asking nothing more than for the governments of the world to address seriously the issue of global multilateral disarmament, we frequently had random objects hurled towards us from passing cars, usually accompanied by wild shouts. We were the target of bottles, cans, contents of ashtrays, remnants of drive-thru meals, etc. A few truckers swerved deliberately towards us, honking their horns angrily.

The favourite all-purpose insult was: *GET A JOB!* I wasn't the only one stung by this, and we sought ways of bolstering our fragile self-esteem against these insults. Back in Washington DC, about a dozen or so peace-marchers had crammed, standing up, into the open back of someone's battered pickup truck – illegal but exhilarating. We were on our way back to our church hall from a concert given by Bright Morning Star, a group of activist-musicians, to a packed liberal synagogue. Matt started to sing one of the songs we had just heard:

'Our life is more than our work, our work is more than a job'.

Everyone joined in with gusto. Those of us like me, Matt and Ellen, who had given up thoughts of jobs and careers for this work of peace – this life of shifting community, hope, longing and material poverty – were roaring out these words at the summer night sky to affirm each other and ourselves in the choices we had made. The song petered out as we forgot the words of the verses, and we bathed luxuriously in the humid summer air, rippled by the forward motion of the pickup truck.

Jack, an ex-merchant seaman in his fifties who had been living rough before the march, was wounded more than most by this vexing imperative towards wage-labour. Jack had a fiery temper and would sometimes trade insults and threats with his tormentors. This would land him in hot water with the monks, who would impose a period of 'purdah' on the miscreant. He would have to walk one hundred yards or so behind the march and be on his best behaviour, though he was never refused food and a bed. To help him keep his outbursts in check, Jack made up a song to the tune of the 'Star-Spangled Banner', the words being: 'Get a job lazy bum!', repeated over and over to fit with the tune. A few of us who also felt undermined by the abuse would join in singing this lustily whenever someone directed the tired old cliché in our direction. It made us laugh and really did help.

We encountered a handful of organized demonstrations against us. Pennsylvania had generally given us a warm welcome, but as we crossed by the coast just south of New Jersey, we encountered Rev. Carl McIntire, a radio preacher, and about thirty of his supporters. They turned up outside St Michael's elementary school in Tullytown, where we were to spend the night, carrying placards reading 'Christ not Marx', 'Freeze Now May Mean Slavery Later' and 'Red China kills Christians', while the good reverend stalked up and down with a bullhorn, denouncing our godless danger to all that Americans hold dear. He was dark suited, with aggressively short hair and a stern countenance, and his female supporters wore horn-rimmed glasses and headscarves pulled tight to keep out unwanted thoughts. Their men looked like insurance clerks and second-hand car salesmen. The local paper reported the event and quoted McIntire: 'These people are using the glamour of prayer and a few songs to conceal the fact that without strength, we will not survive. You can't ignore the evils of communism.' One of his supporters added: 'It's awfully peculiar the Catholic Church is entertaining Buddhists. They're not even Catholic.' Hard to argue with that, though as we weren't Marxists or Chinese or Soviet stooges, it was all a bit confusing.

This night's stop was notable for something else – something wonderful and life-enhancing, in direct contrast to the poisonous bible-bashers. I don't remember when I first saw Karen, but the first time we spoke stays with me as a clear mental snapshot. It was on the landing of a concrete school stairwell, with green-painted iron banisters and railings. She was wearing a navy-blue 'nuclear freeze' T-shirt, jeans and trainers and had joined the march the day before with three friends, after the end of term at their Mennonite College in Kansas. I was going up the stairs and she was coming down. We stopped and spoke. Other people passed us, but in my mind we are alone, frozen in time, as we fell in love on that prosaic stairwell with the Rev. McIntyre's bullhorn in the background.

Later, after we had rolled out our sleeping mats some distance from each other on the floor of the school gym, finding a space among the hundred or so bodies, we couldn't sleep. Several of our fellow marchers were snoring – however, the main reason for our wakefulness was the huge dose of love-adrenalin we had mainlined earlier. We found ourselves making eye-contact and communicated an agreement to get up and leave the room so we could talk. Clumsily weaving through the narrow channels around the sleeping islands, we giggled together after being shushed and tutted at. Out in the sweet, moist, heavy air, we meandered round the car park, pouring out our hearts and souls to each other.

As we talked, the thunder circled us tightly and the first splodges of rain brought out that heady dusty-tarmac smell. We ran back to the sheltered entrance of the school to watch the storm. The lightning was on a scale that I had never seen before, with great sheets of intense crackling light to accompany the boom-boom thunder and the cool relief of rain. We kissed briefly and tenderly and went back to the hall and our sleeping bags for a few hours of ecstatic, yearning non-sleep. From then on, each night we put our sleeping bags down next to each other.

A week later, we walked into New York City across the wooden Brooklyn Bridge. What a way to enter one of the world's great cities – perhaps in 1982 the world's greatest city. It was a wet and blustery early June day, our multi-coloured cagoules and ponchos giving the appearance of determined tourists eager to reach a must-see site. The monks, of course, did not wear waterproofs. They marched, as they had for seven months and three thousand miles, bald-headed and saffron-robed, banging the drum and chanting Na-Mu-Myo-Ho-Ren-Gay-Kyo. I glanced around for the few others who had walked the whole way from LA. Thomas the American Buddhist, who had been my contact back in Kansas City, walked ramrod straight, looking determinedly ahead, not missing a beat – his zeal for Buddhism strengthened by the experience. Paul Owns-a-Sabre, in cut-off denim shorts, T-shirt and bandana, carried the banner as he often did – a proud Lakota, gifted native artist and survivor of frost bite to the face as the march had crossed the Midwest in winter. He had been part of a march for Native American rights six years ago. His anger at the terrible fate of his people and his continuing pride in them were never far from the surface of this great man, and I could feel these emotions radiating from his rain-streaked bronzed face as he challenged onlookers to respect our march. Jo, who had led the dumpster-raids in Washington, skipped along, her whole lined, weather-beaten face a smile. She flicked a continuous stream of Churchillian victory/peace signs to all and sundry.

I was in awe of these extraordinary, tough people. I had walked eight hundred miles in eight weeks, and I was very glad that we were nearly there. I was still a relative veteran compared to the fifty or so who had joined since Washington, who had the energy to take turns with the drums, shout to astonished onlookers and chat and laugh amongst themselves. I was hanging on, one foot in front of the other, determined not to weaken at the last. The rain eased and we stopped for lunch in a local park. As usual, wooden bowls were passed round and food shared out, always an eclectic mix of what

Fig. 6. New York – the Boots have been replaced by trainers at last

we had been given. As usual, there was always some humour from the monks as they called for people to sacrifice themselves and finish the food, as nothing that had been given in kindness could be thrown away. I was so good at sacrificing myself that I actually put on weight, despite walking at least sixteen miles a day!

After the food, I learnt a new trick from Shantha, the smiley Sri Lankan monk. There were no toilets in the park and, now we were in the city, nowhere obvious to pee discreetly. There was a rose bed surrounded by a lowish hedge. We got behind the hedge and Shantha got really low by stretching one leg out straight and as far as possible, bending the other at the knee. He was out of sight now and watered the flowers. I copied his actions, but I was much taller, less flexible and wobblier. My goal was accomplished, but not without drama as I toppled mid-flow and Shantha roared with laughter, attracting curious glances.

I took off my battered DM boots that had now worn through to the sole of my right foot. My blisters there had mostly healed, but

I had a new blister on my left heel. I put on my thin-soled trainers for the last half-day. I felt much lighter straight away. I found a rubbish bin and held a short, but heartfelt thanksgiving ceremony before stuffing the boots in. They had served me well, but I was glad to see the back of them.

The final afternoon of the march was a short walk through a mostly black area. As in previous towns and cities, we got our best reception from African-Americans. Their collective memory of the civil rights struggles meant that our ragged band evoked instant empathy. Shabby men loitering on sidewalks shouted encouragement, housewives stopped chatting and clapped us as we passed them on the street. Walking has great symbolic power in the struggle for peace and justice. It is the most democratic form of transport, the only one available to the poorest of people. It is a properly non-violent way to promote peace, and though most of us were white, it was the ordinary black Americans who saw straight away what we stood for and treated us with respect. We arrived without ceremony at a community hall in a run-down area that would be our base for a few days until the mass rally at the weekend.

Saturday came and it was time for the mass rally. To think that I nearly hadn't come to the USA because I hated the Reagan administration and everything it stood for! On this day, in June 1982, I was part of a one million strong mass of humanity calling for peace. At least ninety per cent of those people were Americans. I remember thinking that when I got back to Europe, my fellow peace activists would find this hard to believe – I was finding it hard to believe myself. One million people. We thought two hundred and fifty thousand in London was impressive, but a whole million people, in New York City, calling for peace... It was a crazy, heady, celebratory day. I had walked eight hundred miles; I had fallen in love and now I knew I wasn't alone. What strength one million people could have. What work for peace one million people could do. Linda Ronstadt, yes, *the* Linda Ronstadt, led us singing Holly Near's great anthem: 'We are a gentle angry people, and we're singing, singing for our lives.'

As we left Central Park there were marchers still arriving – seven or eight hours of a solid mass of peace demonstrators. Surely the world's leaders would have to respond to this huge outpouring of desire for peace.

9

Blockade the Bombmakers

Our peace march was over. The monks and their supporters said goodbye and prepared to go back to Japan. Other marchers went straight back to their jobs and families.

Two days later I took the subway to Lexington-Third Avenue to be part of around one thousand people blockading the UN missions of the five nuclear armed powers. In my honour, our group went to the British mission on Third Avenue. I was with my good friends from the World Peace March, Matt and Juli, together with half-a-dozen fellow activists from their hometown of Columbus Ohio. As a foreigner who risked deportation, I was a support person for the affinity group. It was busy as we emerged from the warm, smelly safety of the subway. There were police everywhere, mostly standing solidly with big bellies straining at leather belts, hands on hips, near their baton and gun. We split up to get around the wooden barricades. Down a side street I saw dozens of police vans, including a bus full of helmeted riot police.

I felt joy, a sense of possibility that we could make the politicians sit up and take notice. But I had never been a natural rebel. I had been more used to trying hard to please my parents, working hard at school, being respectful and afraid of authority. I had been head boy at school, captain of the team – a pillar of my community. So, as the police arrived, two for each demonstrator, I was sweating and shaking involuntarily – my back muscles tensing violently, causing sharp gasping pain that literally rooted me to the spot. My childhood experiences of being bullied had left me terrified of physical violence and confrontation. When I saw the big, burly, armed policemen unceremoniously drag my friends away, hidden emotions from my childhood flooded back into my body.

There had been the bullying on the streets – which often took the form of holding us against our will, like a cat toying with a mouse – whilst home was not always a safe haven, as I had to negotiate the intense sibling jealousy and hostility from my older brother, Pete, and my domineering and fiercely disciplinarian father. It wasn't the actual physical pain resulting from the escalation of a friendly wrestle to a sly punch or a hefty slap around the head for being 'cheeky' that hurt me, for this was generally slight and short-lived. It was the sense of powerlessness against the threat of overwhelming force, at home, on the streets and in the park, that messed with my emotions.

I had to endure a year-and-a-half of this when I spent four terms boarding at my grammar school, when Dad went to work in France. Many old grammar schools had a small boarding house attached, left over from the days of Empire and foreign postings. Ours had been mostly used by the county council for bright boys from difficult family backgrounds (which in those days seemed to mean either a single parent, father in prison or step-parent who didn't want junior around) and by service families. Of course, this meant that they were a rough bunch, and I was, once again, forced into close proximity to older lads (at thirteen years of age I was by far the youngest) who were looking for weaker people to take their frustrations out on.

The first problem for me, apart from the homesickness and loneliness, had been that I was not only younger, but needed much more sleep than the others. I would go to bed only to be woken by the rest of them coming to bed much later, turning the lights on (not lamps but bright ceiling lights) and rampaging about for ages. I soon started to suffer from severe sleep deprivation. I would forget things, lose concentration and fall asleep in class. If any of the teachers noticed, I just got a sarcastic earful rather than any concern.

'I see that the finer points of the structure of the eye are not holding you, Savory,' barked Mr Knight, our aggressive, red-headed, rugby-playing Biology teacher. 'This is a Biology lesson, not a bedtime story.'

He got the laugh he wanted from the other boys and my eyes prickled with tears as my face flushed red. I really missed my Mum. Back in the boarding house, the others, always quick to sniff out a weakness, started calling me 'Zombie' instead of my normal nickname, 'Savers'.

I was discovering that boarding school, like the Army or prison, means that that there is no privacy at all. One evening in this first term, I arrived back at the boarding house from Scouts to find most of the inmates downstairs in the big communal dining/living rooms. The lights were on and, on the dining table, Dowd, one of my dorm-mates, was prancing about wearing my black suede shoes and green bomber jacket whilst the others cheered him on. I experienced a weird sense of violation. These were the only clothes that I had that were not chosen by my parents, and they were being used to mock me in some strange way. Later in the term, two of the sixth-form boarders stole my bike, mucked about on it and buckled the wheel badly enough to make it unusable.

In my second year, there were only four of us left as the council prepared to close the now uneconomical bearding house. Chris, one of the pair who had broken my bike, was over six foot tall, well-built and three-and-a-half years older than me. It was the Autumn term, and I was making myself a coffee over by the kitchen.

Chris shouted over from the TV area: 'Make us a coffee Savers.'

This wasn't an isolated incident, and I decided I was not going to be his skivvy for the rest of the year.

'Make your own coffee,' I replied, returning to sit down.

He picked up a hardback book and hurled it at my lap, knocking my hot coffee all over me. I sat there, frightened, with my trousers and pants soaked as if I'd pissed myself with boiling hot urine. I never felt safe around him or the other eighteen-year-old Steve, who one day, out of the blue, attacked me with a snooker cue and gave me a black eye for eating too slowly.

My first serious direct action taught me just how important it was to train for. If you've never taken part in an illegal political action, you probably don't realise the strength of feeling it unleashes. Sure, I had done the day of non-violence training and read the theory. Even so, I was totally unprepared for that moment, when our truth was confronted by the massed ranks of the New York Police Department and my body went into spasm. During my time as an activist, I often wondered why so few people were willing to take direct action. One of the reasons, I realised, is that many people carry with them the same fears that I did from childhood. Many still experience bullying, violence and arbitrary authority as adults – in the home, at work or on the streets. We are often ashamed of admitting these fears and put on a brave face to the world. Taking part in direct action risks bringing all these emotions to the surface, and it is frightening.

After the protesters had all been detained by the police, an impromptu court was set up in a large school gym and the hundreds of arrested protesters were brought, one by one, in front of a judge. Most pleaded guilty to a minor misdemeanour and received a small fine and were free to go. A few, who either refused to give details of their identity or who pleaded 'not guilty', were detained longer. My group was brought forward and a red-headed woman called Barbara declared that her name was: 'Madeleine Flowers from Kalamazoo'. She was believed, and therefore escaped scot-free.

Outside on the street, after the group had all been processed, we hugged and giggled at Barbara's brass-neck. We spent one more night in Greenwich Village, sitting up until the early hours drinking wine and re-living the drama of the day. I didn't tell anyone about how I had felt, in case they thought I was a coward.

In the morning, Karen and I started travelling back across the US to her home in Fresno, California. Apart from some work for the local Nuclear Freeze group, campaigning took a back seat for a couple of months. It was a hot sunny summer and I was in love. Of course, it wasn't all idyllic. I found myself illegally outstaying my visa, knowing only Karen, and unable to drive. Her Mennonite family didn't throw me out but didn't exactly embrace me either.

As the summer progressed, I became embroiled in a terrible quandary. Should I go back to England, to Bradford and the Peace Studies course, or should I try to stay illegally in California? I was starting to experience bouts of depression, which seemed incongruous in this beautiful setting. I had cut myself adrift from the anchors of my childhood – family, friends, sport, studies and the expectation of a successful but conventional middle-class life, and had no idea how my future might unfold. These dark moods that started to descend on me, seemingly from nowhere, were a new and disturbing phenomenon.

Mum and Dad had expected me back at the end of June, when my six-month visa ran out. It was now July. I had written to them and told them about meeting Karen. They asked for her family's phone number and we arranged a call. It was mid-afternoon in Fresno and the temperature outside was nearing 100 degrees. I was standing nervously in the kitchen, waiting for the phone to ring. In their letter to me, Mum and Dad had expressed their concern that I would stay in America and be physically as well as emotionally cut off from them. I let the phone ring three times and, with a slightly shaking hand, picked up the receiver.

'Hello, it's Chris here.'

'Are you all right? When are you coming home?'

'Hello Mum, I'm okay thanks. I've been wondering about whether coming back to university is the right thing.'

'Oh, Chris, don't throw away another chance. How old is Karen?'

'Twenty – what does…'

'Oh, she's just a girl. When you said you had met a woman, we thought she was going to be much older, maybe with children.' As always with Mum, it wasn't my politics that really upset her – in fact she wanted peace as much as anyone – but my personal life.

'Why don't you come back, go to Bradford, and if you and Karen are serious, well, you can work something out? And anyway, what do her parents think about it all?'

'They're not too keen on me, but I just don't know, Mum. Studying doesn't seem so important at the moment. Being involved in the peace movement feels real. It feels like it's what I should be doing, and I'm in love with Karen.'

'But it's Peace Studies that you have chosen, surely that's going to help you?'

'Hello Chris, Dad here.'

'Oh, Hi Dad.'

'Seriously Chris, we think you should come home. Your visa has run out and you've got your place at Bradford to come back to. You've got friends and family to see again.'

'Okay, I promise I'll keep thinking about it and I'll write soon.'

'Just remember, we love you Chris,' said Mum.

'Thanks Mum, and thanks for ringing.'

Karen managed to obtain a year's placement at the Resource Centre for Non-Violence in Santa Cruz – an institution that had been set up and funded by Joan Baez. They didn't take foreigners on their programme. We were in the living room of Karen's parents' house, sitting on the floor listening to a record.

'Where do you think you'll stay in Santa Cruz, Chris,' Karen asked me as she looked at the carpet and wound a lock of her curly black hair round and round.

Dumbfounded, I said: 'I kind of assumed that we would find somewhere to live together.'

I never for a moment realised that she hadn't thought that we would set up home together if I did stay – I didn't know anyone else and of course was staying illegally. This moment tipped the balance and took me back to England, back to Peace Studies and Bradford.

10
I Ain't Gonna Study War No More

By staying as long as I could in California, I'd left it late to find accommodation in Bradford, arriving in the city only a few days before the start of term. When I called into the university accommodation office, however, I was fortunate to find another mature student in the same boat as me, and we teamed up to rent an ex-council house on the Buttershaw estate. Mary was a down-to-earth ex-journalist and an easy housemate.

When many of the inner-city slums of industrial Bradford were demolished in the 1950s and '60s, the council replaced them with large estates atop the ring of hills that surrounded the old city. They had fresh air (by God the air was fresh!), bigger houses and grassed areas between the buildings. They were also isolated, bleak and like small towns without any of the facilities. Our new home was on the north-western edge, a 1970s addition.

On only our second night in Buttershaw we were woken by violent bangs and the sound of breaking glass accompanied by flashing blue lights. It was three o'clock in the morning and Mary and I emerged simultaneously onto the landing, groggy and anxious to see what was happening. We stood in the dark, peering out into the street whilst remaining partially hidden.

The middle-aged copper was shouting: 'Calm down, mate, you're not going anywhere.'

This was true, as he was sitting astride the bloke's legs whilst his younger colleague was trying to cuff the angry, florid, cussing man who was struggling hard to free himself. The younger copper got an elbow in the face.

'You bastard!' he screamed, grabbing a handful of hair and cracking the miscreants face against our garden path a few times until he stopped fighting back.

Now securely cuffed and bleeding profusely from the nose, this victim of police brutality was unceremoniously bundled into the back of the panda car.

So, this is what it's like up North, I thought to myself. I was badly shaken by seeing such violence close-up. Next morning, I could see the bright red blood splatters across our path and the pavement outside, whilst two doors up I could see a boarded-up front door with its glass panes smashed.

It was an unsettling welcome to Bradford, but my sympathies for this 'victim of police brutality' disappeared as I learned more about the incident. The couple who lived in the house with the boarded-up door had, it transpired, a relationship that consisted of a regular pattern of bust-ups and reconciliations, mixed in with heavy drinking and short banishments for the man.

What broke my heart, though, was the fate of this couple's son and his best mate, who befriended me in the two months that I lived there. Davy was thirteen-years-old with long, wavy, dark black hair and would often be seen barefoot around the estate. His pal Ian was two years older, skinny with angrily-erupting acne. They didn't spend much time at school and clearly craved some adult male attention.

We chatted in the street a few times and then they started to call round to see if I was home. If I was, I'd invite them in for tea and biscuits. The first time they entered our sparsely furnished abode, Davy was shocked to discover that we didn't have a TV. It was such an alien concept to him that he kept on asking me about it, never quite believing what he was hearing. He had a television at home and a video player to boot – but then again, I had shoes…

Ian was clearly a bright young lad and good company. He got bored at school, because secondary school is boring – especially if you are clever and more inquisitive than your classmates, who often conspire to make any progress painfully slow. So, he became frustrated and started mucking around. The teachers couldn't see past this behaviour to his intelligence, or understand that he needed to be stretched and not punished. Ian ended up in a special unit, full of thugs and pupils with unrecognised learning difficulties. This proved worse than ever for this sensitive young man, who soon stopped going to school at all. I was happy to give these lads some of my time, but I wished I could do more.

Mum and Dad came to visit me on the first weekend in November, hoping to find me settled on my new course. They arrived from Essex mid-afternoon, and it was already getting dark after we'd had tea.

From the upstairs of the house, high as it was on a hill on the edge of the city, I started to see flames bubbling up at various points on the horizon. It took me a moment to realise that it was bonfire night, but I was surprised by the sheer number of substantial fires blazing. We set off early to drive to a big hotel in the city centre for dinner. The first piece of wasteland we passed had a pile of pallets burning. Three men were dragging an old sofa out of their house and carried it over to add to the conflagration. This didn't happen in Chelmsford or Oxford. We took a detour around the city, keeping to the high ground. On every bit of scrubby grass or waste ground from old industrial buildings having been demolished, there were more huge bonfires. Kids were running around screaming with delight whilst teenagers and adults drank cans of lager and chucked anything flammable they could find on to the blaze. Although it was a clear cold night, the smoke started to cast a smog-like pall over Bradford, with wild orange beacons emerging randomly from the gloom. It was anarchic, exhilarating and scary.

By contrast, the sparsely populated, dimly-lit modern dining room of the hotel, which had its blinds closed to keep out the wild night, radiated unruffled order. We all relaxed a bit after a drink, and Mum asked me how I was getting on. As dinner progressed, parental anxiety revealed itself in questions about whether there was any prospect of gainful employment at the end of the Peace Studies course.

'Well, there is the sandwich year next year, and I hope to be able to find a placement with a campaigning group in the States. With a mix of that work experience, my own campaigning and the course, there should be opportunities.'

I had strong reservations about being at university at all, but I hoped that Peace Studies would deliver on its promise of a mix of activism and study. I had gone to Bradford for interview in the autumn of 1981, but it had been a study week and I didn't meet any students. The lecturer who interviewed me painted a very positive picture and strongly encouraged me to apply. What I didn't know was, that earlier that year, there had been a full-scale student occupation of the department, and this had resulted in a massive rupture of trust between students and staff. What I had actually found – but not mentioned to Mum and Dad – was that the year group of students I had joined were completely disillusioned with the course, hardly ever turned up to lectures, and did not participate in seminars. The staff, in turn, were unhelpful and hostile and the whole atmosphere was poisonous.

This was destabilising and difficult for me, but on the other hand I was convinced that I was now on a lifetime's path as an activist, whatever happened at Peace Studies. Mum and Dad gave me a lift home before going back to stay in the hotel for the night. I was glad to have seen them and we parted company on reasonable terms.

The main heating in my house was from a large gas fire in the lounge-diner. When it stopped working, we rang our landlord Mr Singh from one of the few working phone boxes on the estate and he turned up three days later with an electric drill. Mr Singh had the bright idea that drilling multiple holes in the plywood facade of the fire would get extra air into the system. Unsurprisingly, this frightened the life out of me. Mary and I resolved to move out rather than face being blown up.

I wasn't going to miss the life-threatening three-mile bike ride downhill to the university, over potholes big enough to charge admission to – nor the lung-busting rides home at night in the wet and cold. After one such journey, I got home, flung my clothes on the bedroom floor, hopped into bed and slept for ten hours in the cold, damp bedroom. When I got up and started to dress, as usual in yesterday's clothes, I picked up my vest off the floor and found that it had blue-grey marks all over it. It had gone mouldy overnight! Nor was I going to miss the pack of feral dogs that roamed the estate and terrified me on a regular basis. However, I would miss Davy and Ian. I felt bad telling them that we were moving out. I wanted to give them something to say sorry. I didn't have much, but I gave Ian my Kodak Instamatic camera and Davy my modest coin collection. I guess I had the forlorn hope that these might spark an interest in them and give them something to do to keep them out of trouble.

Despite the problems on my course, my time in Bradford was full of learning opportunities, even if many of them happened outside the university. Two months on, Buttershaw had acted as a crash-course in Sociology and Social Policy. I then took a practical module on Feminism.

Peter Sutcliffe, the so-called Yorkshire Ripper, was arrested in 1981 for the murder of thirteen women and the attempted murder of seven others. One of his last victims was Barbara Leach, a student at Bradford University. When I arrived in the city, the fear that these terrible events had engendered was still palpable. Sutcliffe had not been caught and this prolonged period of terror had scarred the whole community and had left many women fearful of going out at night. Bradford was an old industrial city, full of terraced houses with dark back alleys. There were also great swathes of the city which consisted of empty factories, demolition sites and patches of wasteland. It could be an unsettling and eerie experience to walk around after dark, even for a big athletic man like myself.

The student union organised minibuses to ferry female students home after events and there were regular 'Reclaim the Night' marches organised by women's groups. These were held to promote solidarity and to question the generally accepted advice that, in order to keep safe, women should keep off the streets at night. Feminists pointed out that women would be safe on the streets if instead men were told to stay at home.

One winter weekday I was walking home from the university between six and seven in the evening. I had to cross two dual carriageways and walk alongside one of them for about half a mile. There were blocks of flats set back from the road, with the carriageway on the left. I walked along this stretch in the dark, completely alone. As I approached the subway that I needed to use to cross the road, a bus pulled up about fifty yards away. A single passenger alighted. She was wearing a long winter coat and high-heeled boots, which clip-clopped as she walked down the stairs of the subway. As I reached the bottom of the stairs, quiet in my rubber-soled boots, she was only about ten yards ahead of me. She must have sensed my presence and looked over her shoulder. She saw a big scruffy man with a beard, a black donkey jacket, dark woolly hat and big black boots. Her face showed her fear. She hurried on, her breath now audible, in short gasps, alongside the rapid clicking of her heels. I stopped walking and said:

'Don't worry, I'm not going to hurt you.'

I was shaken by this experience, as I had terrified an ordinary woman on her way home from work by simply being a man.

The tables were turned at a Christmas party given by one of the final year Peace Studies students at her flat after the end of term. Mandy was tall and good looking with short silver-blond hair. She was also clever, funny and a down-to-earth Yorkshire woman. She seemed to know everyone. Her council flat had a large lounge, which was softly lit for the occasion and filled with smoke and soul music. There were probably twenty women and half a dozen men there. An hour or so after I had arrived, I was in the kitchen chatting to a few people when there were suddenly raised voices from next door. I could see a group of leather-jacketed, big-booted newcomers entering the flat. Many had short spiky haircuts, but the leader who was over six feet tall, powerfully built and with long, straight brown locks.

The party had been crashed by a dozen or so lesbian separatist-feminist bikers, who were demanding that it should be a women-only event. Mandy was furious with them but unable to throw them out. She apologised to us and made it clear that men and straight women were welcome to stay. I lurked in the kitchen for another hour before ducking out and away. On the long walk home, I realised that I had learnt an important lesson in how it feels to be excluded from something on the basis of a characteristic that can't be changed. These events, combined with daily conversations with feminists and reading feminist theory (particularly Andrea Dworkin's *Woman Hating*) fully converted me to the radical feminist cause.

11
You Can't Kill the Spirit

The one practically useful module that I was taking at Peace Studies was about the arms race. We learnt important background, including geopolitics and military strategy, as well as all the relevant facts and figures. This stood me in good stead for the countless discussions and arguments I was having about nuclear disarmament. I had already studied campaigning tactics during the cold and lonely weekends at the beginning of the year whilst in the US. I had carefully read Gene Sharpe's seminal book on the theory and practice of Non-Violence in the town's public library. I used Sharpe's ideas to plan how I would approach campaigning when I returned to England. I imagined myself as a non-violent Lenin in exile. Now was my chance to put this into practice although, unlike Lenin, I had precisely nil followers.

At the time in Yorkshire, there was a strong feeling that the Peace Movement was too centralised and London-dominated. So, I chose a local focus for action: the USA communications base at Menwith Hill, on the moors outside Harrogate. It was run by the shadowy United States National Security Agency and was their Northern European centre for intercepting and monitoring telephone, radio and satellite communications. As such, it was (and still is) a potent symbol of British subservience to the Americans and the infringement of our civil liberties, as well as a crucial cog in the American nuclear war machine.

I wrote to all the thirty or so Peace and CND groups in Yorkshire suggesting a meeting to launch a campaign of Non-Violent Direct Action (NVDA) against Menwith Hill. This was typed, clumsily and slowly, on an old portable typewriter, photocopied and stuffed into envelopes, addressed by hand, and finished off with stamps paid for out of my student grant. The crucial point was that the campaign should try to embed itself in local communities, as opposed to focussing on the actual physical site itself, and slowly build ordinary people's willingness to act. British Telecom was still in public ownership and I proposed a set of low-risk actions to highlight BT's role in the phone-tapping and to generally publicise this secret base that undermined British civil liberties. I wanted this to appeal to more than just convinced peaceniks and to broaden out the concept of direct action from sitting in the road or climbing fences. This could have included, for example, paying BT bills on special cheques that objected to their involvement in Menwith Hill. We could also sticker phone-boxes, do street theatre and die-ins[2] at Post Offices, work with the relevant trades' unions and fill-up MPs' surgeries with activists. The theory was that this would build public knowledge and involvement, so that when we did go to the base and block the entrance or trespass inside, we would have public opinion behind us. This was vital if we were hoping to actually achieve our aims rather than simply make a noise.

Thirty-two people came to the first meeting on Saturday 19 February 1983, from groups all over Yorkshire. Marion, an American non-violence activist and trainer, came over from Leeds and took on the role of facilitating the meeting. The participants were all active members of local peace groups, mostly middle-aged and in employment. This was better than I could have hoped for.

However, despite my caveats about peace camps in the invitation letter, this was the most popular idea at the meeting by far. It was really the only idea that had support, probably due to the high profile of Greenham Common. Not one of the other participants at the meeting wanted to join me in my step-by-step approach – maybe I had explained it badly or lacked the charisma and authority to take people with me. Maybe Lenin would have suffered the same fate if he had suggested paying taxes on special cheques rather than seizing the Winter Palace and shooting the bourgeoisie!

In the late 1950s and early 1960s, most disarmament-related civil disobedience was in the form of sit-down protests in central London. The focus had now shifted to military bases and other significant places involved in the preparation for nuclear war.

---

[2] Die-ins were a perennial favourite in the 1980s. Essentially, a group of people would lie on the floor somewhere public whilst other activists, often dressed in white overalls and gas masks, would survey the destruction wrought by a nuclear attack. Passers-by would be leafleted and engaged in conversation.

This strategy had the advantage of allowing local groups all over the country to find suitable targets for action in their own areas, highlighting the huge US military presence in our country and publicising spy-bases, bomb factories weapons-storage facilities, nuclear bunkers and other civil defence installations as well as airbases. The disadvantage was that most of these places were deep in the countryside and protests were not seen by many ordinary citizens. There were logistical problems as well relating to transport, food and toilets.

Despite the enthusiasm for a peace camp at the meeting, no one wanted to set up a permanent presence at this bleak moorland site. Instead, it was proposed that the different local peace groups would fill a weekend or two each and keep up a camp for one weekend a month for as long as possible, with a bigger protest planned for the Saturday nearest 4 July, which was to include some direct action.

Meanwhile the first Yorkshire-wide NVDA was initiated by a group from Leeds CND. They suggested a mass trespass at Easingwold in North Yorkshire. This was the site of the bunker that North Yorkshire County Council would operate from in an emergency, and it was also a college for training staff from around the country in civil defence. We took a mini-bus and a couple of cars from Bradford and were around eighty strong at the protest. In the event, we were able to walk straight in to the site and hold a tea party outside the locked front doors. Group consensus prevented a few hotheads from trying to break into the buildings and after a couple of hours of being observed by a lone security patrol, we left and went home. A local radio reporter turned up and I was able to put our message out on BBC Radio Yorkshire. Non-violent revolution was proving duller and more difficult than I had imagined back in St Joseph.

Away from protesting, a momentous event had occurred in my personal life. I had seen Amanda around the university as she was in the first year of Peace Studies, but we hadn't really spoken much. Then, her birthday coincided with a departmental disco. Despite being shy, I had inherited my Mum's love of dancing and had the chutzpah to be the first up on the dance floor. The room was crowded around the edges and the music was hotting up. I took the plunge and started moving to some Bob Marley. I skanked on my own for a good two minutes before a couple of others joined in. Gradually, more people lost their inhibitions and the dancing really got going.

John Lennon's great love song *Woman* started, and I found myself slow dancing with Amanda. We were both hot and sweaty from dancing but held each other close as the beautiful music and the sadness at John Lennon's recent death filled the room.

We went outside in the dark to cool off amongst the concrete maze of the university buildings. We talked and then, after getting cold in the late November night, went back inside. I had been too shy to read the signals and to kiss Amanda. She told me later that she had had her eye on me and had engineered our going outside together. Of course, I was still attached to Karen, and waiting for her to come to England the following Easter. I convinced myself afterwards that I had already decided in my heart that in the long run it wasn't going to work with Karen. I had become frustrated that she couldn't understand what I was going through in Bradford, with Peace Studies being such a disappointment. Her cheery letters jarred with my growing frustration and feelings of being lost and alone. The truth, I suspect, is that although I was feeling more distant from Karen, being propositioned by a pretty, sexy, confident young woman was too hard to resist.

A few days after the disco, there was a meeting of the Yorkshire and Humberside Ecology Party in Bradford. I went along and was surprised to see Amanda there. We were the only two young people attending, out of a group of about a dozen. We sat together and formed a radical alliance against the old fogies who ran the Party.

After a day of sitting close together, supporting and defending each other, we went back to her room in the university halls of residence and made love. We then spent most hours of most days together for the next ten years.

The last night of 1982, this tumultuous and extraordinary year for me, was not spent boozing and partying and singing 'Auld Lang Syne', but freezing my butt off in the Oxfordshire countryside. I had come down from Bradford to visit family and friends in Oxford over the festive season, but being a peace-activist was a full-time occupation, and so I had made sure that there were also some actions I could take part in. The main event was a blockade of USAF in Upper Heyford. New Year's Eve was chosen for the symbolism of starting the New Year as we intended to go on: working for peace and nuclear disarmament. USAF Upper Heyford was one of the biggest and most important American airbases in Britain and it was home to a squadron of long-range bombers, with significant nuclear capacity. The plan had been to create a human chain round the entire airbase and, in doing so, to block all the entrances and exits.

Amanda had come down after her family Christmas in Yorkshire to join me and we arrived at Upper Heyford in a minibus from Oxford at around six in the evening. It was already very dark, and the cloudless night sky sparkled with stars that warned of a seriously cold night.

With good local knowledge, our group from Oxford had chosen to block a country lane that was the only route to a rear entrance of the base. Our driver had taken a circuitous route in order to put the police off our actual intentions, and the plan was to get out of the bus quickly and double back on ourselves in order to block the road before the cops had cottoned on to our destination.

The driver turned left at a crossroads and then stopped suddenly. We exited as fast as possible but were slowed down by the bulk of our clothing and boots. Finally we were out, and we started half-running, half-walking back to where we wanted to block the road. A group of four or five coppers saw what we were doing and moved to intercept us. It was like a grown-up game of British Bulldog. The police couldn't cover the whole width of the lane, so they targeted individuals, letting others slip past. I was close to the verge on the left of the lane, and a burly sergeant, red-faced and wheezing, shoulder-barged me. I fell awkwardly into the two-foot deep ditch by the side of the road. I was unhurt but shocked at being assaulted by a member of the constabulary. The police soon gave up though, as most of our group had got past them, and they had clearly been briefed to not make unnecessary arrests. I got up and scurried down the road to join the group. This was the first and only time that I was assaulted by the police. I could easily have hurt myself badly as I fell. My youth and fitness and my many layers of clothes no doubt helped prevent any damage.

This activity had got the adrenaline flowing, and for about an hour we were high on the success of evading capture and successfully blocking the road. However, we began to realise that actually no traffic was trying to get past us. A messenger was despatched to find other groups and bring back news. It transpired that in order to avoid conflict, the commander of the base had decided to close it for the night once everyone was in or out after seven o'clock. There had been more activity at the main gate for an hour, but not enough protestors to effectively block the gate, which kept a significant police presence to clear the way for vehicles.

We now had to stick it out until after midnight on our own. We kept our spirits up by singing peace songs and received a welcome hot drink from a support car. From ten o'clock onwards we were getting very cold as the thermometer plunged to well below freezing. After midnight, we walked a couple of miles to the pre-arranged pick-up point and were delighted to see our minibus approaching. Piling in, we started to thaw out, and convinced ourselves that it had been a worthwhile exercise. A small success – and the best thing was that, after we got dropped off at Oxford station to walk back down the Botley Road to our friends and fellow eco-activists Jon and Jenny's house, a newsagent had left an *Oxford Mail* poster outside: 'Peace Protesters close Heyford Base' it declared. Not entirely true, but a great souvenir.

We woke up on New Year's Day 1983 with the news that around forty to fifty women had broken into Greenham Common whilst we were at Upper Heyford, and had managed to get onto a silo. A picture of them dancing on top of this stark symbol of war made headline news and became an iconic symbol of our struggle. They were arrested and a special court session was convened in Newbury for them to face charges on New Year's Day. Jon took us down in his VW camper and we hung around outside the courthouse for a couple of hours. The crowds grew steadily, and we must have numbered over 200 when the women started emerging. Wildly whooping, cheering and hugging we sang the Greenham anthem, over and over again with pride:

You can't kill the spirit, she is like a mountain, old and strong, she goes on and on, on and on.

Our movement was growing stronger by the day. CND membership was exploding and opinion polls showed small majorities in favour of 'Refusing Cruise' (missiles). More importantly for me, CND was officially embracing Non-Violent Direct Action (NVDA) as a legitimate tactic, and a string of large-scale actions were planned for this New Year.

So, I started 1983 full of hope.

12
Loneliness and Love

Back in Bradford in early January 1983, I discovered a widespread rash on my upper body. The doctor at the university health centre diagnosed German measles and I had to be quarantined, which was a profoundly disorienting experience. As it was in the days before mobile phones and digital communication, I was really cut off – and of course no one could visit me.

I was released after a week from the isolation unit into a grey, windswept January day. Feeling wobbly and out of sorts, I sat down on a bench near the health centre. Looking over the university towards the city of Bradford, I felt profoundly disconnected from the world. The euphoria of that moment outside Newbury Magistrates' Court had slipped away, and now felt like the distant past. Over the last seven days, I had had plenty of time to ponder my situation, and I had found it impossible to stay positive, despite the growing strength of the peace movement. I was reeling from the disappointment of the Peace Studies course being so far from what I had hoped. I felt a fool for not choosing to either stay in the USA or to go back to Oxford, or even choosing one of the other courses I had applied to – and I felt guilty at having broken up with Karen by telephone over the Christmas holidays. I was deeply distressed at the continuing fragility of my relationship with Mum and Dad. I had hoped that my new relationship with Amanda would make all this better, but despite our immediate and deep connection, we also made each other unhappy for reasons that I didn't understand.

In order to try and re-connect with a sense of my core self, before Christmas I had tried seriously to take up hockey again. I had grown fast as a child and my muscles couldn't keep up, so I never made the age-group football teams, but by the age of fourteen I was able to play centre forward in a men's hockey team. What a feeling it was to motor past a cursing and puffing defence, latch onto the ball round the advancing keeper with a shimmy and sidestep and crack the ball home against the wooden backboard, relishing the thud and then wheeling round to receive the plaudits of my teammates. I began to live for the weekends and the thrill of scoring goals, going on to be a county player. To my horror, I found that the knee pain I had suffered at the end of the World Peace March returned after any repeated pressure, so it stopped me from training. Along with other joint problems I was developing, it prevented me from playing any sport ever again. This was a huge blow, as sport had been such a joyful escape for my emotions. I had been completely obsessed with sports. For every football, hockey and rugby team I played in between the ages of fifteen to nineteen, I was the top scorer – every season. I felt I could make things happen through sheer will power. If I wanted something enough, I could get it. I determined to become Head Boy in my final year at school, and when I was duly made Head Boy, this feeling was reinforced.

Passing exams, scoring goals, being made Head Boy, were all clearly defined and achievable personal objectives. Achieving nuclear disarmament and world peace were anything but. After this attack of German measles, I experienced a deep post-viral exhaustion and serious depression. I experienced an inner darkness that would leave me incapacitated for hours on end as I lay on my bed, curled up with tension and anxiety and overwhelmed by the magnitude of the task ahead of me and the power of the forces ranged against our movement.

In addition to my new worries, I also had an unfillable need for love and acceptance, like a black hole, based on and bequeathed by my childhood experiences. Amanda and I had started going out at the beginning of December, and in February 1983 we moved in together as we now felt inseparable. We never tired of sharing our life-stories with their many similarities, along with softly spoken hopes and dreams, as well as anxieties and upsets. This involved being together in one decent-sized attic room in a terraced house, shared with three other women from Peace Studies. We quickly felt like we had been almost physically joined together.

However, we were both young and unprepared for the consequences of such strong emotions, alongside our political struggles and personal searches for a way forward in our emerging adult lives in a society we felt oppressed by. The closeness of our relationship and contentment togetherness was punctuated by regular sulks and silences and the occasional explosion from Amanda. She seemed conflicted about commitment to one person – it wasn't what she had had in mind when she came to university – and she also had her own hidden troubles.

Early in our co-habitation, in the middle of an argument about me going away for a weekend without her to do some conservation work, Amanda really lost her temper, and I thought she was going to hit me as I cowered on the floor, not understanding what I had done to provoke this rage. After she had left me alone, another emotion took hold: the repressed anger of all the times I hadn't felt able to hit back when I was being bullied welled up and erupted. That anger was also now fuelled with the buried rage of discovering at eighteen that the praise, love and respect from school and home seemed dependant on me continuing to conform.

This rage was stoked at Oxford and now it included visceral anger at governments and their plans for nuclear war, along with the repression, torture and conventional wars being waged against ordinary people around the world – rage against inequality, injustice, sexism, racism and ecological destruction. I couldn't direct this anger outwards, so I slammed my head against the wall again and again and then I punched myself in the head and punched the wall.

I shouted incoherently: 'I've always tried so fucking hard. Why isn't that enough? What more could I do? Why is everyone so fucking angry with me? You lied, you've told me big fucking lies – war, poverty oppression – it's caused on purpose – lies, lies more fucking lies!'

My own pain and the pain I felt for the suffering of others, my own anger and the rage I felt towards those in power, my own fear of violence and my fear of nuclear war, were all tangled up together.

It was the combined strength of these feelings about myself and about the world that had led me to take such an extreme path. These feelings were a powerful motivator and they allowed me to take risks that most people were too afraid to take. However, the emotional consequences of that risk-taking – leaving Oxford University and my old life behind for the life of a full-time activist – were only just starting to become apparent. I had not realised just how difficult it would be to hold on to a robust sense of self-worth. I had cut myself off from the people and places and activities that had given shape, structure and direction to my life. I wasn't getting any pats on the back for what I was doing – often quite the opposite. Every day was a huge struggle to keep going forward. I did, however, despite all this, still find reserves of energy and drive that I could call on to start up more groups, organise more events and blockade more bases.

13
A Second Helping of Greens

Bridlington in November 1982 was the unlikely setting for political intrigue. The Ecology Party Autumn conference was being held at the Winter Gardens, in this once popular seaside resort on the east coast of Yorkshire. I opted for the budget accommodation, which meant sharing a 1950s chalet on a deserted holiday camp. My friend and mentor from Oxford, Bookshop Jon, had asked me to write a radical defence policy for the party, based on what I was learning at Peace Studies. I duly obliged and proposed a policy based purely on defence that mixed defence-oriented conventional forces with organised non-violent civilian resistance, or Social Defence as the German Greens had called it.

Jon and a small group of like-minded friends were orchestrating a coordinated attack on the conservative strands of Ecology Party policy. As the conference progressed, they scurried around the hall, whispering in corners, rushing off to type out and copy alternative proposals and compromises. I stayed in the hall waiting for my big moment when I would speak in favour of my paper. Every half hour or so, Jon would rush up with a freshly-minted page of re-writes in order to seek my approval.

I had inspired my friend big Sam from Lady Margaret Hall to join the Ecology Party and he had come up for the conference. I was delighted to see him, and we popped outside for regular roll-ups and chats about Oxford and all the people we knew back there. He was now in the final year and doing interesting work on Indian politics. I felt a stab of regret and envy.

Back in the hall, I stood at the podium in front of the two hundred delegates and made a passionate appeal for the Party to adopt my policy of radical disarmament and gradual de-militarisation. I thought, but didn't say, that we hadn't got a hope in hell of being elected, so we might as well adopt the most radical polices we could.

Sam, Jon and I and a few other radicals stayed in the bar until closing time, drinking creamy Yorkshire beer and smoking. Our conversation alternated between moaning about the number of conservatives in our ranks and plotting the next stage of the Green take-over of the party. I stumbled back to my chalet in the murky sea-fret that had descended, getting lost for a while among the identical wooden sheds, and then fitfully sleeping off the beer – waking up later, dry-mouthed and jaded.

My contribution to a published book, *Nuclear Free Defence*, showed that I wanted to revolutionise society by persuading the majority of the population to turn away from militarism, patriarchy and capitalist consumerism, and to embrace internationalism, feminism and eco-socialism – rather than win local council elections by being cautious so as not to offend. For example:

Modern industrial society and weapons of mass destruction are inseparable partners. The 'defence' industries and the arms trade are just the most obvious links. The values that underpin an exploitative, de-humanised, violent mode of economic production make modern militarism possible.

I was thinking about my stint on the production line in St Joseph here, and how workers in a weapons factory would be much like my colleagues there: decent enough individuals but cut off from their feelings about the end result of their work.

In Germany, the Greens were getting plenty of media coverage and were involved in many direct actions against nuclear power, airport expansion and nuclear weapons. In 1982, the party split, with the more conservative ecologists forming their own separate party. One February Saturday morning in York, at a meeting of the Yorkshire and Humberside Ecology Party, Amanda stormed out tearfully when the chairman insisted on staying the chair*man* and would not consider being called the chairperson or chair.

'I am a man, and proud of it, not a piece of furniture,' repeated Stanley, the retired bank-manager, to my back as I hurried after Amanda to support her.

This incident reflected in a microcosm the divide in the Ecology Party between relatively socially- and politically-conservative conservationists and scientific ecologists on one side, and on the other political- and social-radicals who were inspired by the German Greens and embraced direct action, feminism, gay rights and eco-socialism.

Fig. 7. My Green badges

The conservative side held sway and so I abandoned trying to modernise the Ecology Party and instead set up a Green Group at Bradford University, quite possibly the first one in the country. I started by inviting David Taylor, who had initiated the Green Gathering movement, to speak at a meeting on 23 February 1983. He readily agreed and I put him up for the night. We made a collection at the meeting to pay his train fare. In the event, the room I had booked was on the small side as forty-six people from a wide range of departments inside the university, and a handful from outside, squeezed in to hear David's inspirational message. With his long blond hair, blue eyes and sensuous lips, David spoke from the heart, making eye-contact with as many of the audience as possible. At the end, there was a sustained ovation that sent shivers down my spine. We were on our way. The new group immediately started campaigning for the University to make 'greener' decisions in waste disposal, energy and financial investments.

Fig. 8. leaflet from 1983

Around this time, I teamed up with Dave Farrar, a local Bradford Ecology Party member, to plan our very own Green Gathering in the city. I took on finding and booking the visiting speakers and did this from the phone box near my house on Barkerend Road. I used to save up all the change I could, take a notebook and pen with all the numbers I wanted to ring, and wait my turn to use the phone. Many of our neighbours didn't have phones at home, so the box was popular, and sometimes I would go out three or four times in an evening and still fail to find it empty. So once in, I resolutely made my calls, using up my carefully-hoarded supply of loose change, despite sometimes having to face down the impatient and hostile stares from the queue outside. In the end, I managed to book a wide range of speakers, from as far afield as the Scottish Highlands and the Isle of Wight, to talk on a mix of practical subjects, like bee-keeping and vegan cookery as well as more politically-oriented ones that focussed on non-violent direct action in the pursuit of disarmament.

Fig. 9. Me at The Bradford Green Gathering, 1983

Dave and I conducted our meetings in the Karachi curry house, his favourite. It was down the end of a street of terraced houses that came abruptly to a halt where a new dual carriageway had cut through. A very unprepossessing spot for a business, the restaurant was mostly patronised by local Pakistani families. I was a vegetarian, and it is fair to say that the vegetable curry was poor, consisting of tinned mixed vegetables in a curry sauce – but the onion bhajis were divine – perfectly balanced between onion and a light crunchy batter. You could also watch the chapattis being cooked over a single gas flame that looked like a Bunsen burner. They were fresh and delicious and were used to eat the curry with, instead of cutlery. Then the *pièce de résistance* was a milky coffee with Burfi, sweets made from evaporated milk. It was these meals that fuelled the Green Gathering.

The Gathering took place over the weekend of 25-26 June 1983 at the university. An amazing 1,100 people participated. The organisations, stallholders and speakers who attended were almost universally positive. The Bradford Green Gathering put green politics on the map in the city and influenced neighbouring towns and cities too. It had been our idea – Dave's and mine – and we had gathered together a small group of half-a-dozen others to create this fabulous event, working happily in a non-bureaucratic way and with no hierarchy. The Gathering spawned a regular Green newsletter and a green jobs initiative.

One of the cornerstones of Green thinking is that we should try and live out our ideals in our everyday lives. For me, this included volunteering for conservation work, helping out on organic farms, growing my own vegetables where possible, and living a very low-consumption lifestyle. However, lifestyle, as politics, is never as straightforward as it seems. Many activists in Britain turned to vegetarianism or veganism in the late 1970s and early 1980s for political reasons. My main reason was a response to the argument that large-scale food production from animals was wasteful of resources, and that a plant-based diet would allow more people in the world to have sufficient food. I have never believed that it is morally wrong for humans to eat other animals, but I have always supported a high level of animal welfare. Unfortunately for British vegetarians, most of the food that we started eating came from much hotter countries. The staples of brown rice and pulses, such as chickpeas and kidney beans, soya-based products like tofu and miso, as well as tahini, peanut butter, dried fruit and nuts for our muesli and olive oil, all had to be imported. For a true eco-warrior, this brought up the dilemma of the 'food miles' attached to this diet, with the implications of fuel and resource use. I had become a proficient vegetarian cook by this stage, and friends would enjoy coming to eat at our house. I was bothered by this reliance on these far-flung ingredients, and decided to investigate local solutions. I experimented cooking with whole wheat grains and whole barley grains, as an alternative to brown rice. Both these cereals took a considerable time to soften in cooking. Pulse replacements were much harder to come by. The climate in the UK was just not warm enough to ripen beans and peas sufficiently for drying. The only exceptions I could find were marrow-fat peas, used as mushy peas to go with fish and chips, and field beans, a type of broad bean used generally as cattle fodder.

I managed to get a packet of field beans from a wholefood shop and invited some friends round to sample my really 'right-on' recipe of field bean and barley stew, flavoured with home-brewed beer and marmite. The beans and barley were soaked for twenty-four hours in cold water, then brought to the boil, soaked for an hour, drained and boiled again, with the beans having the additional encouragement of being pressure-cooked. Meanwhile, I sautéed onions, garlic, carrots and swede before adding some marmite dissolved in the beer. The field beans were added to this great vat of vegetables to stew. The table was laid for two friends from the university, along with Amanda, me and two of our housemates. I tested the barley. It was still tough. After another whole hour of boiling and tasting, we were impatient and hungry and so I dished up.

The flavour wasn't bad, but the beans were as tough as the proverbial old boots. The barley was edible but taxing on the jaw muscles. Alex and Linda, our housemates, ate a small amount before declaring themselves full. Amanda braved a whole plateful. My two pals and I, all hungry young men, got stuck into seconds. One friend, unbelievably, had thirds.

It was uncomfortable, but not so unusual, for a vegetarian to have a bit of rumbling after a high fibre meal. As we sat round the table chatting, the farting started. One after another, we let rip with trouser-ripping intensity. It was like a field of sheep grazing on turnips. This recipe was never repeated and has been passed down in folklore as a warning to future generations.

It's clear that during my time in Bradford I was very much an instigator and motivator who got things going, who was able to inspire and lead people, and in fact had some considerable success, particularly in Green politics. So why couldn't I really enjoy and celebrate these successes, feel good about myself and use it as a springboard to prominence in the Green political world? It was pretty clear that I wasn't going to have a conventional career, although becoming a national figure could have given me a boost in self-esteem and energy.

Part of the answer is that I was deeply suspicious of leadership ambitions in myself or anyone else. From my school experience, I had discovered that people often proposed me for leadership roles. I knew that, if I did certain things, it would be relatively easy for me to achieve some sort of prominence. However, what had pushed me towards my life of activism was a burning desire to do the *right* thing – the morally-correct course of action – rather than to pursue personal ambition. The second, more complicated part of the answer is to do with me being white, male and educated. I was aware of the importance of not getting in the way of women, ethnic minorities and working-class people from taking on leadership roles. The world didn't need another white man telling everyone else what to do. There was also an element of self-hatred and self-flagellation in this way of thinking. I was part of the problem, so should suffer some punishment. So, I stayed committed to local activism. As the fledgling Green movement had very few local strongholds, and none in the North of England, I started to lose touch with it.

14
Stand Up People, Make Your Choice

Easter 1983 was earmarked for a blockade of RAF Burghfield in Berkshire, which was not an air base but a factory that had made the nuclear missiles for Britain's current Polaris submarines, and was gearing up for the manufacture of warheads for the new Trident system. The factory was situated near Reading, but secret enough for the MOD to keep it off the Ordnance Survey map – and close enough to Greenham Common and Aldermaston (the nuclear weapons' development facility) to be part of a three-cornered protest.

Amanda and I had teamed up with five other students from Bradford to form an affinity group for this blockade. The language and techniques for NVDA had emerged from the USA, from the civil rights movement and humanistic psychology, via the

Fig. 10. We love life! Burghfield, 1983

Quaker-inspired Movement for a New Society to the anti-nuclear power protests in the late 1970s. I thought that these structures and processes for effective group-work, and for building a lasting movement of non-violence, were excellent. They encouraged open and honest communication about practicalities and emotions, emphasised mutual respect and inclusiveness, and were designed to create strong bonds and the possibility of a continuing commitment to non-violent action, despite the dangers and difficulties. The strong emotions felt by all of us who were prepared to take illegal action and suffer the consequences, could also be destructive in the absence of a safe place to express them. One of the issues that peace movements face is that many of those drawn to them (like me) are actually full of anger. That is why proper and sustained training for NVDA is so important.

During the action, the affinity group would most importantly stick together and look out for each other. This blockade was set to last for three days, so getting on well and looking after each other was vital.

There is a recurring theme from my accounts of NVDA – the cold! Camping at Easter, and spending hours on end sitting in the road, required my tried-and-tested layering-up technique and a lot of foot stamping and complaining. The layers for me consisted of thermal

Fig. 11. Sitting in the road at Burghfield

vest and long-johns; one pair of thin socks and one thick; tracksuit trousers and thick cotton shirt; two jumpers; dungarees over the top; leg warmers; scarf, woolly hat and gloves, and boots... Fully dressed, I looked like an overweight mutant offspring of a brickie, clown and '70s disco dancer. Again, the authorities decided to let us block the roads for a few days, rather than create a confrontation with thousands of people. Our preparation for arrest was not tested, only our endurance and willingness to repeat this activity again and again.

After the blockade of Burghfield on Thursday 31 March 1983, and the peace chain between Aldermaston, Greenham and Burghfield on the following day, Amanda and I made a mad dash cross country to get to the middle of nowhere in Cambridgeshire. It was worth it for such a happy event. Friends of ours and fellow activists from Bradford, Tim and Bridie, were getting married in two ceremonies: one at the Quaker Meeting House in Leicester and one at the peace camp on the base at RAF Molesworth. Bridie was from a well-established Quaker family in Leicester and a nurse, and Tim was an American Quaker who had come to Bradford to do the MA in Peace Studies.

The base at Molesworth had been completely abandoned more or less, and there was no military presence except for a small waste disposal centre. There was no effective fencing and most of the site had grown wild.

A People's Peace Camp was set up at Peace Corner, on Old Weston Road by the wartime entrance to the base, on 28 December 1981. The camp was initiated by the Fellowship of Reconciliation, during a pilgrimage from Iona to Canterbury cathedral. A simple multi-faith chapel, Eirene (Greek for peace) was built in spring 1982. Tim and Bridie had the idea of using the derelict land on the base to grow food to send to Eritrea, where there was a terrible famine, and gathered some other like-minded folk to camp at the base and help to start the project.

This project was in its very early stages as we joined some other friends and activists camping on the base to celebrate their wedding. A joyous and life-affirming ceremony and a good sing around the fire were followed by an early night. We slept very well and woke surprised at the how dark it still seemed in the tent. On opening the front zip, we soon discovered the cause of this – a centimetre or so of snow covering the fly sheet and right across the flat heathland of the deserted base. This created a magical landscape that added to the sense of hope which had been created by the love and spiritual depth of the wedding ceremony.

A couple of months later, we travelled down to Oxfordshire for the next big CND set-piece blockade, which was to take place between 31 May and 3 June at Upper Heyford in Oxfordshire. This was an ambitious national event to block the base, over several days and nights, at a time that would be inconvenient for the authorities to ride out by simply closing it down. It was fully expected that this would lead to mass arrests. I had been prepared for arrest at each direct action I had taken part in. The prospect scared me, and each time I had to find the courage and emotional strength to take that extra step to do something illegal. I never felt that I was a romantic rebel taking on the powers that be. I didn't enjoy the butterflies in my stomach before sitting down in the road outside an airbase. I didn't enjoy the confrontations with the police or service personnel. I didn't relish the prospect of being roughly bundled into the back of a police van and locked in a cell. I had a deep fear of prison and the powerlessness and potential of violence that it represented. Having said this, it was also a weird anti-climax each time we were allowed to block a base all day, or were moved on without arrest. This time it really did feel like we would finally face the consequences of breaking the law.

Amanda and I joined a different affinity group from the one we had been with at Easter at Burghfield, a mix of students and working people. For once, we went through proper non-violence training from an experienced facilitator – Howard. He was confident enough to get rough with people when role-playing a policeman. I hadn't seen this before and people got upset. One man ended up grappling with Howard on the floor. When we all calmed down, we had the most genuine discussion I had ever had about our fearful and angry feelings when faced with violence.

Four years later, I wrote the following in an article for *Peace News*:
My deep anger about what is happening in the world is mixed up with the personal anger I feel from being treated with disregard, disrespect, contempt and from being subjected to violence, both during my everyday life and during my peace actions. I hate physical

violence, I go to jelly and feel sick when it happens around me, or to me. I have never taken my anger out on others less powerful than me, so I have taken it out on myself instead.

So, when I take part in a non-violent direct action and I suffer abuse or violence from the police or others, I don't just see them as policeman, I see them as my father, brother, headmaster, as the bullies from my past. I also see them as the strong arm of the state which has enormous power over me. I have 25 years' worth of anger against strict authority and bully boys, 25 years of fear to deal with. I feel like I'm too angry to act non-violently and too afraid to act at all.

And when I have tried to talk to people still active in non-violent direct action about my feelings, I have largely come up against moralising disapproval of my angry and violent feelings. People seem to want to suppress the feelings rather than try to deal with them.

What I didn't say at the training session, or in that article, is that I now felt less of a man because, as a child, I had never fought back physically against the bullies. A real man would surely not be afraid to stand up for himself with his fists? The more I was involved in non-violent action, the more I was tormented by these feelings, replaying in my mind childhood confrontations and changing them to scenarios where I gave my persecutors a good hiding. I think you will understand why I believe that, for non-violent action to be sustainable for individuals in the long run, thorough and sensitive preparation is vital.

However, despite these issues, the support for direct action was growing, and groups from all over the country agreed to join a rolling blockade. Amanda and I went down early to Oxford to see friends and family. The rest of the Bradford contingent travelled down by minibus in order to arrive in the early hours of the morning on 1 June to be part of the Yorkshire group action taking place between 6 a.m. and noon.

Amanda and I took a train and bus to the base later than planned, due to a night disrupted by upset stomachs. We couldn't find our mates from Bradford, despite tiring miles of walking around the perimeter base. We eventually discovered that they had all been arrested taken into custody in the early morning, the very moment they had sat in the road. This time, the authorities had decided that they *would* keep the base open. Amanda and I found a few other stragglers who had lost their original groups, and we all sat in the road. After a while, we were warned that we would be arrested if we didn't move, which is what duly happened. We were manhandled to the grass verge, but then the policemen who arrested us realised there were no vehicles available to put us in – they hadn't returned from taking the last tranche of blockaders away.

'Wait there,' a passing inspector ordered.

We did as we were told for about two minutes, but then – realising we were unguarded – slipped away. We repeated this trick three more times. We were about to try it a fifth time when we saw a red double-decker bus approach the stop outside the base. We hopped on the bus back to Oxford for much needed sleep. This is how I came to be arrested, but didn't have to go to court. In a way, I was disappointed to have missed out on the badge-of-honour of a court appearance, but excited at the size and success of the action. With general election coming, I was hopeful that, in a week's time, we might have a government committed to nuclear disarmament.

15
Stand Down Margaret

Mainstream politics butted back into my life on 9 May 1983, when Prime Minister Margaret Thatcher called a snap general election to be held exactly a month later.

Despite a surge in her popularity after the Falklands' war, Thatcher remained a hugely divisive figure and many people loathed her and everything her government stood for. One of the highlights of my time as a student in Bradford came near the beginning of my first term – a gig by The Beat in the student union. This chart-topping ska band filled the thousand or so capacity hall to bursting, and we danced exuberantly all night to their irrepressible, high-tempo music. Then, at the end, they played the second side of their double A-sided number one hit. The radio stations all played 'Mirror in the Bathroom' but loads of people bought the record because they wanted the other track: 'Stand Down Margaret'.

As they launched into this rarest of beasts, a political pop song, the students' union hall erupted. There were wild cheers, whoops and shouts as the dancing got more frenzied. I, like everyone else, was going crazy, sweating profusely and pumping my fist in the air with all my might. 'Stand Down Margaret, Stand Down Please, Stand Down Margaret.' They finished to immediate bellows of 'More, More!' So, they played it again and finally a third time. Sweat and condensation ran down the walls of the hall as the lights came up to reveal a thousand, happy, red-faced, beer-fuelled Thatcher-haters. Six months later, they were nowhere to be found as the election campaign got under way.

One of my housemates, Linda, was a member of the non-sectarian Alliance party in her home city of Belfast, and I was an Ecology Party member who had campaigned for the Liberals at the last general election. However, both Linda and I thought it vital that under Thatcher the Tories should be stopped, and this was a chance of a lifetime to elect a pro-disarmament government (the Labour manifesto pledged the cancellation of the Trident nuclear programme and the removal of Cruise missiles from Britain). So, we volunteered to work for the Labour Party. We found a disorganised local effort in place with very few party members to help with the campaign, and despite our efforts helping leaflet the Thornhill estate and canvassing all-round the Leeds Road, the Tories won a second parliamentary term with a large majority.

In the early hours of the morning, as a bunch of our housemates and friends huddled round the portable black-and-white telly in our lounge, we discovered that the Conservatives had even won Bradford North, our constituency. The anti-Tory vote had been split three ways, between the official (Militant) Labour Party candidate, the de-selected sitting MP and the newly formed SDP. On that fateful night, I realised the huge significance of the result. The post-war social-democratic consensus was smashed, and the prospects of a pro-disarmament government had gone for a very long time.

Amanda suddenly leapt up from the sofa and, without saying a word, pulled on a coat and hat, grabbed a can of white spray paint and slammed out of the house. I followed as she stormed down the road. We came across a house with a 'Vote Conservative' poster in the window. It happened to be an end-terrace with an accommodating side wall. Amanda set to work spraying abuse along the lines of 'Tory scum not welcome here'. Another house got similar treatment and then we reached the HQ of the local Conservative party. This got the rest of the contents of the can, inviting the Tories to 'Fuck off out of Bradford North'. I was getting increasingly nervous about being spotted by a police car and so was delighted when the can ran out of paint and we were able to run back home. This petulance had relieved a little anger, but we knew that it didn't disguise the fact that this was a serious and significant defeat.

Bradford North had been a safe Labour seat for donkey's years. The incumbent MP had angered left-wing activists through his alleged inactivity in opposing Thatcher and his alleged expenses-paid trips to apartheid South Africa. He was targeted for de-selection by Militant – they wanted to put this particular donkey out to pasture. By accident, I came to know much of the detail of this process through my friendship with the notorious Earl Billheimer.

Earl was an American who had been a Democratic Party activist at the 1968 convention in Chicago, when leftists and anti-war activists were brutally attacked by the police. This had radicalised the young man, who decided that he needed to fight fire with fire. On arrival in England, he found a welcome home among the Militant Tendency.

We met on the top deck of the 31 bus going down Barkerend Road to the dole office. This was after the election when my grant money had run out and I had officially left Peace Studies. I was a university dropout waiting until the autumn for the chance of a fresh start. Earl and I had to sign on at the same time every two weeks, and we soon became firm friends. Earl was delighted to have an intelligent conversation with someone outside the Labour Party that he could talk freely with, and I loved his anecdotes and wickedly-dry humour. He wasn't shy about telling me how Militant had manipulated the rules to take control of the local party: keeping meetings going on until late at night until everyone else went home; changing times and venues of meetings at short notice to put people off; and gradually intimidating others to leave committees through verbal and personal attacks and hints of physical violence.

The *Daily Mail* got to know about Earl and his activities and printed at least two articles attacking him, one with the sub-heading: 'Earl Billheimer cannot vote in Britain… but he has influence. Man from Chicago helps in sacking moderates from the Labour Party.' I didn't approve of his methods at all and was appalled at the consequences of a Tory MP for Bradford North (for the first and only time), but there is something glamorous about an outlaw – especially a clever, funny one who likes you.

Bradford, however, was a bitterly divided place in the aftermath of the election and, as my time on the Peace Studies course petered out in disillusionment, I was badly in need of some R & R in the countryside.

16
Festivals, Friendship and Failure

In 1983 there was a wide range of free meetings, Green Gatherings and music festivals to choose from to help restore the energies of the jaded activist. Amanda and I hitched from Bradford to Glastonbury in mid-June. We got stuck in Bristol and walked miles through the city. We were carrying all of our camping gear on our backs, and as the evening progressed we were getting tired and anxious about where to spend the night. Salvation arrived in the form of a bunch of friendly old hippies in a VW camper van. They were stocking up on scrumpy at an off-licence in the suburbs when we saw them and asked for a lift. They took us all the way to the festival and we put up our tent in the dark in an empty field. When we woke up ten hours later, we were surrounded by a sea of brightly-coloured nylon. We had woken up because the sun was shining fiercely, and we were suddenly unbearably hot and sweaty in our sleeping bags. We crawled out of the tent for relief but found that the temperature had soared into the '80s Fahrenheit. My hay fever kicked in with a vengeance, and I sneezed, streamed and wheezed my way through the weekend. No one was expecting such good weather and the festival site glowed at night from the tens of thousands of bright-red, sunburnt bodies.

The Green Gathering late in July, also held near Glastonbury, was to provide more serious medical problems. First of all, the gathering had been crashed by the Convoy. This was a large group of New Age Travellers, who lived on buses and stuck together for support, fun and safety. They were receiving national media attention as they toured the country, upsetting locals and challenging the police's authority. Opinions were divided amongst the more mainstream Greens at the gathering. Some were attracted to their freewheeling spirit, whilst others were concerned about the drug use and undercurrents of violence. I was torn between these two points-of-view until we woke up on the second day of the gathering to find that our food, cooking stove and utensils – that we had stored under the flysheet of our tent overnight – had been stolen. It became apparent that it was the semi-feral children of the Convoy who had taken our things, because they were not getting properly fed by their parents. We had to buy meals that day from the food stalls that had set up around the field.

The next morning, I woke up feeling generally unwell, without knowing quite what was wrong. Amanda left the tent and returned with some watermelon for breakfast. It was delicious, but I still felt strange. One of our neighbours was a healer and she offered to help. She produced a crystal on the end of a cord and proceeded to dowse me for the cause of my ailment. As she put her hand on my stomach and swung the pendulum in front of me, I projectile-vomited bright red watermelon about ten feet across the grass. Then the runs started. I felt too weak to leave the tent despite the uncomfortable heat and hard ground, so I resorted to using plastic carrier bags (rule number one of camping: you can never have too many plastic bags). Then Amanda was sick. In the morning, Oxford-bookshop Jon drove us to Glastonbury station. We somehow managed to get to Oxford without public embarrassment and were rescued by big Rip Bulkley – who I first knew from Oxford CND but had recently joined the MA in Peace Studies at Bradford, where we had become friends. He drove us back to the comforts of his large North Oxford house. I had never been more grateful for anything in my life than the wonderful cool crisp sheets, clean tap water and peace and quiet. We went to the Bulkley's GP's surgery and I had to crawl the last fifty yards up the road as I was too weak to walk. We had heard from Jon that morning that there had been an outbreak of dysentery at the Green Gathering. However, the doctor would not believe that he could ever have any-one at his practice with dysentery, so he just advised us to stop eating for forty-eight hours. Tests later proved him wrong. After five days of fasting, I tried a dry piece of toast and the whole wretched busi-ness started again. It was to be at least ten days before we could start eating again. Two weeks later, back home, Amanda suffered a sec-ond bout of dysentery. We properly understood now why people in poorer countries died from such diseases and how lucky we were to have clean water and proper sanitation, even on the dole in Bradford.

We had recovered enough to go to one last festival that summer at the end of August, the Green Moon Festival in Nenthead, an old lead mining village high up in the North Pennines of Cumbria. We hitched there from Ripon surprisingly easily (after visiting Amanda's parents) and put up our basic two-man tent, which had a pole at each end and a fly sheet that didn't cover the front or back. We were on a bit of a slope up above the tented village, where the food and craft stalls and marquees for meetings were pitched on the only flat ground.

It was a small, friendly gathering, more interested in new-age spirituality than politics, and held in a spectacular setting. On the second day, it started to rain heavily late in the afternoon. We were down in the tented village and sheltered in the biggest marquee along with sixty to seventy others. The rain persisted and small rivulets began to form in the grass, snaking downhill. We were all getting a bit bored with just standing watching the rain when a skinny, bearded guy in his thirties took off all his clothes, produced a bottle of shampoo and walked out into the rain and took a natural shower, to great applause. Eventually we decided to get back to our tent to make some food, lie down and see out the storm. After a while, it became clear that our shelter was not coping adequately with the extreme conditions and water was finding many and varied ingresses into our mini-home. We stuffed our bedding and clothing into black bin-bags and sought refuge in our next-door neighbour's bigger tent.

They were a couple of weekend hippies from Manchester, working in normal jobs but enjoying the freedom of festival lifestyle during weekends and holidays. They generously found room for us to sit and plied us with red wine. We shared a spliff or three. Earlier in the afternoon there was just rain, but now there was thunder rolling round the valley with shockingly loud and scary explosions of sound. The spliffs help calm us down, but all four of us were hoping it would end soon. The storm continued to bounce around the surrounding ring of hills and stayed very close. Interspersed with the thunder were searing flashes of lightning, illuminating our flimsy nylon shelter. Then suddenly the ground shook, as I imagine it would in a small earthquake, people screamed, and we could smell burnt, damp earth. Our host scrabbled with the infuriating tent zips and opened the door. Outside, the occupants of the tent on the other side of ours had literally been flung out of it by a direct hit from a lightning bolt.

Distressed and confused on the wet grass, the man clutched his left arm with his right one, saying over and over again: 'I can't feel my arm; I can't feel my arm.'

His partner whimpered but was too shocked to speak. We helped them get into their car to keep dry and took it in turns to stay with them. After an hour or so, the feeling returned to the man's paralysed arm and they packed up in five minutes, chucking everything in a bundle into the back of their estate car, and fled.

When the storm finally subsided, I went to look at our tent. The smell of burning earth was still strong and I discovered that the lightning had hit both tent poles, front and back, and had burnt a sizeable hole in the ground at the base of each. We could easily have been killed if we had been squashed into this small tent, quite possibly touching the poles by accident, as the lightning struck. I took our sleeping bags to our neighbour's tent, and we spent a fitful night in their living area.

The summer of festivals had not turned out to be the sun-kissed, care-free period of relaxation and fun that I had hoped for, and now we were back in Bradford for the winter, a gloomy prospect. We had one ray of sunshine in our lives, though. Our next-door neighbours were a Pakistani family with two of the most adorable little girls you could ever hope to meet, Asma and Sima. Looking for things to do whilst their mother was busy, they started to come around to our house. They were comfortable with us because of the large female contingent in our house, I think. They were only four and two but could already pitch in and help with laundry in the bath and chores in the kitchen, as well as running about giggling and bringing some uncomplicated joy into our lives.

Along with woodwork, typing and local history classes, I looked for a positive campaign to get involved with. The occupation (Work-in) of Thornton View geriatric hospital, Bradford, began on 5 August 1983 in response to plans by the local health authority to close it down. It was an eighty-two bed, long-stay geriatric hospital located near the village of Clayton, just outside Bradford, and for most of the elderly patients it was their home. As long as there were patients in the hospital, workers could not legally be locked out or lose pay during an occupation of NHS premises.

The staff were extremely busy looking after the patients and managing the hospital, and so needed other people for the picket line and to be an extra presence in case the authorities tried to force entry. I spent many afternoons there over the winter in the porter's lodge, ready to repel intruders who never arrived. In the end the occupation, which lasted twenty-one months, fizzled out, with the authorities playing a waiting game, as elderly residents died and no new ones replaced them.

Naturally, we went down to London again for the CND national march and rally in October 1983, and it turned out to be the biggest of them all, with an estimated 400,000 people attending. I was starting to feel alienated from the middle-class, woolly-jumper mainstream marchers, who would go back to their nice houses and to their jobs on Monday morning. At the time, I couldn't understand how they could feel moved enough to come on the demonstration but then be able to compartmentalise their peace-protesting into a small box, as they got on with their everyday lives. I was seeing them less as allies in the struggle and more as irritating dilettantes who, when the chips were down, retreated to their privilege. How could we full-time activists persuade them that, if they were willing to join us in some large-scale NVDA, the movement could actually achieve its aims? If fifty thousand people had sat down outside parliament and refused to move, the debate would have been raised to another level. They took their coaches home to what I enviously imagined to be nice houses, families, jobs and money. I was left frustrated at the failure of this huge demonstration to achieve anything.

I saw this as achieving nothing, because Cruise missiles arrived in Britain from the USA in November 1983. What we didn't know at the time was that November 1983 was also the moment that the world came closest to nuclear war since the Cuban missile crisis of 1962. Documents released in the last few years through Freedom of Information requests, have revealed that a massive and highly realistic NATO exercise in Western Europe caused genuine concern in the Soviet Union, that the West was preparing to attack them. Operation Able Archer involved forty thousand troops moving across Western Europe in response to a scenario where the Soviets had invaded Yugoslavia and then Greece and Finland.

Relations between the two sides in the Cold War were extremely tense. Earlier in the year, US President Ronald Reagan had famously called the Soviet Union 'the Evil Empire' and had announced plans for a 'Star Wars' protective shield to save America from Soviet missile attack. In early September 1983, the Soviets had shot down a Korean Airlines Boeing 747, killing all 269 people on board, nervous that it might be an American spy plane. On 26 September, the Soviet nuclear early-warning system reported that a missile had been launched from the United States, followed by up to five more. Luckily, the commander judged it to be a false alarm and nuclear weapons were not fired.

As operation Able Archer got under way, the Soviets thought it was actually the start of an attack on them and they responded by fitting aircraft in East Germany and Poland with nuclear weapons, placed long-range nuclear missiles on serious alert and sent submarines carrying nuclear missiles to hide under the Arctic ice. Before war broke out, an East German spy managed to convince the Kremlin that it was indeed only an exercise.

If our governments in Western Europe had not kept this secret, the peace movement would have gained massive additional support. Our fears would have been seen for what they were: not as naïve fantasies, but as very real. Regardless of the wider political ramifications of this, it would have been psychologically beneficial to me and other activists. Finding out thirty years later that I was totally justified in my urgency to promote disarmament, can't undo the psychological damage that I suffered from having my truth so resolutely denied by government, the media, people in the street and close family. Some activists built a hard, defensive shell of faith to protect them from doubt. Faiths ranged from Marxism through Trotskyism, Anarchism and Buddhism to Christianity. Without any such defence, I was wracked with self-doubt. Maybe the powers that be really did have the best interests of everyone at heart? Maybe the Soviet Union really was the 'Evil Empire'? Perhaps I had given up the opportunity of a lifetime to study at Oxford University for no good reason at all? As Christmas approached, I realised that I had wrecked my chance of getting any kind of degree. I was living in poverty in the cold, depressed city of Bradford and I was unemployed and virtually unemployable. I very much wanted to be able to find meaningful work that I thought was ethically sound and part of the solution, not the problem. However, first I needed to sort myself out.

17
The Great Escape

After Christmas in Yorkshire, Amanda and I went down to Oxford for the New Year to see Gran, Auntie Pinkie (Gran's twin sister) and our old mates. On New Year's Day, we sat up late talking with Bookshop Jon and he told us about friends who had spent the entire summer cycling round Brittany. Back in Bradford, we were lying in bed on a cold January night when I sat up and said:

'That's what we can do – go touring on bikes around Europe.'

'Yeah, why not, I like it,' Amanda said, immediately enthusiastic.

We then chatted excitedly, deep into the night. Lured by the prospect of sunny days, the open road and new people and places, the idea became a firm plan before morning. We could get away from Bradford, Thatcher and her supporters, Cruise missiles, the rain and the cold. We could also seek inspiration on what to do next, now that we had dropped out of higher education. We would cycle through France to Italy and then up through Austria to Germany and home. We would stop whenever and wherever we liked, for as long as we liked or until our savings ran out. We resolved to move out of Bradford as soon as possible.

Mark, one of Amanda's best friends from Ripon, had his own haulage business and he came down in his van and took us and our bikes up to Ripon. After a few weeks preparation, we left our modest possessions in the care of Amanda's parents, Jack and Mary, and set off to Oxford. We arrived in Cowley at the beginning of May and received the warmest of welcomes from Gran.

'You're as welcome as the flowers in spring,' she said, as she often did, and – like every other time – it felt as if she really meant it. It was always a joy for me to come back to 159 Hollow Way. We were going to celebrate my twenty-third birthday, staying a few days and then off to the West Country to see my new-born nephew Robert, before taking the ferry from Plymouth to France. My birthday treat was a takeaway from the Chinese fish-and-chip shop across the road. Large chips, mushrooms fried in batter with lashings of tomato ketchup washed down with some cheap, sweet, fizzy white wine.

The next morning we said fond farewells to Gran and took the train from Oxford to Bath. We didn't know that Bath was surrounded by long, steep hills in all directions and so our first real leg of the cycle ride was a challenging climb out of the city. Delighted to get to the top, I was enjoying the descent, my extra weight taking me much faster than Amanda, as I accelerated downhill. I was fully laden and travelling at thirty miles an hour on the smooth-surfaced main road. I was in the middle of the carriageway, to stop cars squeezing past, as I took the next bend. It was sharper than I anticipated, and this caused me to swerve further out into the middle of the road than I wanted to. Coming slowly up the steep hill towards me was a bright green single-decker bus. It took up pretty much the whole width of the carriageway on its side the road, with no real verge and only a dry-stone wall that took up the rest of the available space.

I was wrestling the handlebars with all my strength, heading just over the white line in the middle of the road as I made eye contact with the bus driver. His face drained of colour and his eyes were wide with fear. I ducked under the side mirror of the bus and swept all the way down the side, missing the green paint by millimetres. When I could finally get the bike under proper control, I came to a halt and sat on the grass, waiting for Amanda to catch up. I was trembling with delayed shock and terror. I had been so close to death. Amanda found me hunched over, head between my legs, shaking. We stayed there for nearly an hour before I was able to resume.

We cycled and camped through the Somerset Levels and Exmoor and stayed a few nights with Auntie Mabel. She still lived in the ramshackle converted First World War hut near Bampton in Devon, where I had enjoyed so many childhood summer holidays. We then rode across the hills of Devon and Cornwall to St Austell to see my brother Pete, sister-in-law Rachel, and new-born nephew Robert. We took the ferry from Plymouth to Roscoff in bright sunshine and, as we rode off the ferry first, cycling ahead of all the lorries, we received a round of applause from the workers on the dockside.

The weather then turned against us and for a week we had to endure high winds and incessant rain in Roscoff. We battled along the coast against gale-force winds to Plouscat. Here we found that the campsite wasn't yet open for the season. There were, however, ageing but usable toilet facilities on the nearby beach. We pitched a tent in the lee of the closed toilet block on the campsite in order to get some wind protection. The next day we huddled in the tent as the hoops of fibreglass were being blown almost to touch the ground. We had our (vegetarian) bacon well and truly saved by a German couple who turned up in a VW camper van. They had been unable to get to Ireland because the ferries had all been cancelled and so they had decided to stay in Brittany. We sat in their van drinking coffee and playing cards until the worst of the weather passed. Two days later, we scarpered to the nearest train station and hot-tailed it south in search of better weather. We were also on our way to find Marie-Therese who lived in a tipi, deep in the South Breton countryside outside of Redon.

Marie-Therese was a friend of Mark's, the man-with-a-van from way back, who had moved us out of Bradford. She had been a social worker but had decided that she wanted to live as lightly as possible on the Earth and had found a sympathetic friend who allowed her to pitch her tipi in a small wood that they owned. We camped in the adjacent meadow. The weather had turned warm, and the lush, fecund countryside in this forgotten corner of France felt close to a paradise on earth. We were invited to lunch with Marie-Therese and were taken aback to discover that she lived on what she could gather, and what she was given. So, the salad, served from a large wooden bowl onto small wooden platters, consisted mainly of bitter forest and hedgerow leaves, with some grated carrot and raisins. We had bought some bread to share. We stayed for four days and for future meals we cooked pasta, and took bread, cheese, green beans and tomatoes to supplement the foraged salad.

It became clear that the troubles of the world and the cruelties that she had witnessed as a children's social worker had proved too much for Marie-Therese. She had had a breakdown, stopped work, spent time in a mental hospital and had now decided to live a spiritual life in close connection to nature. She had acquired a serenity and an acceptance of fate that I had not met before. The Catholic Worker community and the Buddhist monks I'd been with in the USA were deeply spiritual people who lived simply, foregoing many of the comforts of modern life. However, they were also activists who engaged fully with the world and were supported by a faith community.

Marie-Therese had some loyal friends, but she was getting very thin, and we realised that, alone in a tipi, the cold, damp winters would be hard to survive. Five years later we heard from Mark that Marie-Therese had developed pneumonia and died. I was deeply troubled by my memory of this singular woman with such spiritual strength and yet emotional and physical fragility. How *do* we live with the knowledge of the violence, cruelty and suffering in the world? All of us, at least some of the time, block out that knowledge in order to survive day-to-day. Whole political belief systems are created to justify inequality, racism, war, terrorism and cruel repression. Religious belief systems find ways of containing believers' responses to these realities by encouraging charity and judgemental morality. For individuals like Marie-Therese, who couldn't defend herself against the knowledge of violence, cruelty and suffering, the result is often mental illness, extreme self-sacrifice or self-harm.

Marie-Therese put us in touch with some of her friends, who would also be pleased to meet us. We cycled off to spend the night with Joseph, an anarchist farmer in his early sixties. He was a short, wiry, tanned man with a shock of white hair, restless energy and an irresistible smile. He scraped a living on his small family farm and fought bureaucracy and arbitrary authority in whatever form it manifested. He was currently agitating against the central government's attempt to build a new airport in the Breton countryside (This fight was eventually won in 2018!)

We were made welcome and helped lay out a huge trestle table in the garden in the shade of a row of plum trees. It was Sunday, and along with his wife and mother who lived on the farm, Joseph's children and their families were coming for a Sunday dinner. There must have been sixteen of us crammed around the table on that warm June evening. Food, wine, conversation and love flowed freely. Joseph held court, talking politics, farming and family matters. We were feted as honoured guests, despite being strangers, and after the cheese course was finished, Joseph's elderly mother produced a dusty bottle of her famed plum eau-de-vie. The clear firewater burned down my throat. However, you really could taste the plum, and after the second glass, as we toasted international friendship and the withering away of governments, I was happy to accept a third.

The final member of this magic trio of friends was Chantal, who herself had battled for years against bureaucracy and institutionalised discrimination to become the first – and in 1984 the only – female lock keeper on France's canal network. We arrived in the evening and had the unforgettable pleasure of seeing the sun setting at one end of the canal, and the moon rising at the other. Chantal cultivated a large vegetable garden, kept bees, made honey as well her own yoghurt and cream cheese from milk brought to her to her by a local farmer. When we finally returned to England, this little bit of southern Brittany fuelled dreams in us of rural self-sufficiency and living close to nature. As the trip continued, these dreams became concrete plans to find somewhere of our own – somewhere rural in the north of England, and to find an ethical way of making a modest living.

18
Come With Us!

Through a mixture of knee-related physical frailties and a developing love of the French way of life, progress was slower than we had initially planned. In the end we spent over three months in the west of France, travelling from Roscoff to the Dordogne. It was clear that we were never going to make it across the Alps into Italy, as we had originally dreamt. So, we took the practical step of getting a train from Bordeaux to Stuttgart to visit my cousin Alison, her German husband and two young children.

As we were leaving Alison's in Stuttgart on the way to visiting our camper-van saviours from Plouscat, Helmut and Maria, at their home in Augsburg, we literally bumped into a Peace March, deep down in a Stuttgart U-Bahn station. As we descended to the platform, we were surrounded by a gaggle of scruffy young peace protesters with rolled up banners. It was clear that we were kindred spirits and we soon found a fluent English speaker who explained what they were doing: walking from Mutlangen (one of the two sites allocated in West Germany for American Pershing 2 missiles) to the federal capital, Bonn. It was 11 August and they were on the second day of the march. Their main banner read: 'Stop the War against Humanity and Nature: Come With Us.' So, we did.

After two nights in Augsburg we spent two more with a Servas host in Munich. Along with visits to the Olympic Park and the Englishergarten, we took the opportunity to go to the Dachau concentration camp. A bus from the city centre took us quickly to the site of the camp, which had been restored in part so that people would remember what had happened there. The short bus ride was the first shock. We were close to the city and surrounded by villages. This meant that local people must have known very well what was going on. A bunch of us got off the bus and went into the reception area. Many people had cameras and we were all dressed casually like tourists. Can you make a tourist attraction out of a concentration camp? I was already feeling uneasy. Then

Fig. 12. On the march in Germany

came the shock of discovering that the place had been opened as early as March 1933, as a concentration camp for Communists, Social Democrats and Trades Unionists, as a way of eliminating political opposition. It was another four years before homosexuals, disabled people, Jews, Romanies (gypsies) and other enemies of the Nazis were brought in. As a political activist, I could see that these first victims were people exactly like me.

A beautiful and haunting sculpture formed the centrepiece of the memorial. It looked to me like a mass of humans stretching out their arms and legs and desperately clinging to each other. On the bus back to Munich I thought about the new, more peaceful, more equal society that I wanted to help build. It had to be made by ordinary people, and those ordinary people were some of the same ordinary people who were capable of the most extraordinary cruelty. I still believed in the power of non-violence, but I was disturbed by how easily the opposition had violently been crushed by the Nazis.

We returned to Stuttgart, picked up our bikes and joined the peace march further north in Landau. We progressed steadily north

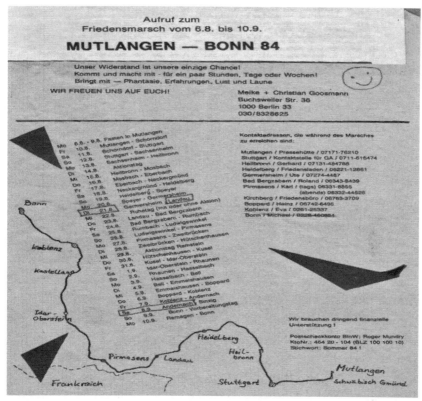

Fig. 13. Peace march leaflet

through the Pfaltz region, a rural area close to the French border, where the US military had been able to build large bases and areas for manoeuvres.

The policing of the march was different from our experiences in Britain, especially as the cops were all armed and their guns were always ostentatiously displayed. We were usually headed by two policemen in a car, followed by another two in another car, flanked by about three on motorbikes and usually tailed by two civil plain clothes police, or *zivvis*, as they were known. Around Ramstein – the biggest US airbase in Europe – and nearby Miesau – the second largest US weapons and ammunition store in Europe – our escort grew to six van loads of police, one of them for each one of us. We spent two days around these bases and were watched from 6 am to 11pm by plainclothes police. They often tried to listen in and see what was happening, and we were constantly hassled by them taking photos of us. Interestingly, they were particularly nasty when we tried to take photos of them, quickly resorting to physical violence and smashing cameras. These invasions of our privacy worried us considerably. Why were they so keen to get multiple pictures of us? What security purposes were they to be used for?

Perhaps because most people on the march were under thirty, and at least half under twenty-five, there was a lot of direct action, with few reservations about illegality. This was quite different to my experiences in the USA and Britain. There was no fussing about the violent aspects of cutting fences, and on one occasion a US Army truck was occupied and the brakes tampered with. This caused a great deal of argument within the march and promises were made not to do anything else that might endanger human life. I am sure that this would have completely split the march in Britain.

In addition to standard peace protests, there were also some women-only actions. The most powerful and scary was at Baumholder, a town with the highest rate of rape in Germany –since the US Army had come to town. It was the most oppressive atmosphere I have ever felt on a demonstration. It was a thundery day and there were dark brooding clouds above. American service vehicles were everywhere, and the occasional group of uniformed GIs swaggered through the town. The locals seemed downtrodden and fearful. When Amanda wrote an account of the protest, she described the town as: '… an Americanised town, full of porn and macho aggression.'

The women stood silently in a semicircle, hands linked, in the town square. They had made a series of placards which they rested against their legs, that linked male violence towards women to the violence that makes war. They began to moan softly, at first for sisters who had been raped. This moaning grew louder and turned into screams of rage at the men who had perpetrated this violence. The townspeople who saw the protest either scuttled past as quickly as possible, or stopped to shout angry words. It felt as if they didn't want to be reminded of the grim facts.

The men on the march, and the women who had felt too uncomfortable to participate, stayed close to the protesters and gave out leaflets explaining what the protest was all about. I was scared stiff. The young women who wailed in the streets had real courage, and I was proud that Amanda took part. The moaning and screaming cut clean through the leaden atmosphere. I felt sick to my stomach. I hated having to contemplate the terrible violence that men all over the world dish out to women on a daily basis, and how rape is used as a weapon of war and occupation.

A later protest at the huge Ramstein airbase also used sound to good effect. We bashed sticks, pans, tin cans and whatever we could find to make a rhythm, hammering out our rage against the death machines behind the barbed wire. The atmosphere that permeates operational military bases, of death and violence wrapped up with secrets and lies, enabled us to get in touch with our deep feelings. I remember wailing, shouting, screaming, mourning, raging and sorrowing. I beat the metal drum with all my puny might. Wanting a world without war is not an intellectual pursuit. Yes, there are countless rational arguments for trying to solve human conflicts without killing each other, but above all, my activism was based on a deep emotional response to the horrors of weapons of mass destruction, mass killing and legitimised violence.[3]

---

[3] A week before this protest, on 11 August, President Ronald Reagan, during a voice check for a radio broadcast, remarked: 'My fellow Americans, I'm pleased to tell you today that I've signed legislation that will outlaw Russia forever. We begin bombing in five minutes.' Great sense of humour, Ronnie.

19
Work, Dole and Gender Roles

After five weeks and 600 kilometres, the march reached Bonn. Amanda and I peeled off to the train station, exhausted. We were desperate for a friendly face, English conversation and a break from cops, airbases and arguments.

With considerable relief, we boarded a train to Bochum, in northwest Germany. We were on our way to visit Ian, a friend whom we had got to know on the Peace Studies course in Bradford, and who had now returned home to Germany. He had decided, like us, that the course was not worth completing. We were greeted at Bochum station by a broad Yorkshire accent and a bear-hug.

Ian had grown up in Yorkshire but had moved with his family back to his Mum's native Germany, aged fourteen. He was jolted into peace activism by the Falkland's War – sickened and ashamed by how quickly the British people seemed to become sabre-rattling jingoists. Amanda and I were planning to join him and some of his local friends at a large scale NVDA against NATO manoeuvres at Fulda Gap.

However, when Henning, a lorry driver friend of Ian's, offered us a free ride back to Blighty, we jumped at the chance. On the boat I was Herr Schmitt, Henning's co-driver, and Amanda hid under the duvet on the bunk in the lorry's cab, so we didn't have to pay for the ferry ride. At Felixstowe there was a problem with the documents for part of the load, and so we spent the night sleeping in the back of the wagon in a secure compound in the docks, with Henning in a bed in a nearby hostel. Luckily for us, the load included boxes of curtains which made beds that were comfy enough. It was eerie and unnerving being locked in the back of a truck for the night but, in the end, we slept well enough and were relieved to hear a cheery Henning banging on the side and wishing us good morning at around 8 am. The immigration official was surprisingly relaxed about our unconventional entry into the country – very different from now, of course. After a few drop offs, we arrived in Ripon at teatime and

Henning parked up near Amanda's parents' house and came in with us for a bacon sandwich.

We had been inspired by our trip and were set on finding useful work and establishing an ethical and community-centred way of life somewhere rural in the North of England. We didn't plan to stay in Ripon, as we knew finding somewhere affordable to live would be impossible. We intended to stay with Amanda's Mum and Dad long enough only to find our own place and start our new life.

However, a visit to the Job Centre threw up a local opportunity. A government scheme to get the long-term unemployed off the dole was creating useful three-day-a-week jobs for a year. The local National Trust property, Fountains Abbey and Studley Royal, was offering conservation and estate work. We could learn some new skills and have something positive on our CVs, and this would make it much easier to move somewhere new in a year's time. We desperately wanted to be independent and able to hold our heads up high, as we paid our own way in society. Alongside protesting against so many things, we wanted to be building a better world, here and now. So, we applied for and were given the jobs.

Amanda and I cycled the three miles to work on our first day. It was a crisp autumn morning, with a hint of frost. I sucked deeply at the damp sweet decay of the air, feeling as usual the promise of new beginnings that I associated with this time of year. The chestnut leaves had turned first, showering the grass with giant red and yellow confetti. It was good to be back home after five months on the road in Europe, and Yorkshire was doing its best to grab my attention and shout: 'Stay here, look how beautiful I am!'

It was also the rutting season for the lucky red deer in Studley Park, some of whom would get to mate in the near future. As we cycled round the first big bend inside the park gates, I spotted two stags facing up to each other around a hundred yards away. One emitted a ferocious, roaring bellow which was returned in kind. Both heads dipped and feet pawed the ground, plumes of hot-breath mist erupting from their extravagantly-flared nostrils. Then, the charge, bone cracking against bone, antlers locked.

This was followed by the clunk of metal against tarmac, and the soft thud of body against ground. I had been moving more and more slowly, transfixed by the raw power of this ritual violence.

Crucially, I had forgotten that my feet were strapped into the toe clips of my bike. I toppled sideways to the ground like a silent movie star. I yelped, Amanda laughed, and the magic of the moment was gone.

We arrived at our base, which was an old caravan next to the tool store. Our leaders, Steve and Mike, turned out to have both been in the military. Would they be able to turn our ragtag bunch comprising North Yorkshire's finest long-term unemployed into a crack working unit? Our official work clothes hadn't arrived yet and, in our old donkey jackets, combat trousers, faded jogging bottoms, saggy hand-knits, cagoules and ripped jeans, we appeared like a bunch of people who had been allowed to take their pick from the unwanted remnants of a jumble sale.

It was the first day of the year-long project, and the eight of us were driven round the estate by Steve, who seemed to find the silence oppressive. So, as well as pointing out the work we were to do, he gave us his life story, which had included a long spell in the South African Defence Force. A pheasant suddenly made a suicide leap in front of the mini-bus. Steve slammed on the brakes, but could not avoid killing the hapless bird:

'Bloody pheasants, just like the blacks in South Africa, fucking stupid!'

Had he really just said this? He had.

It was the first day and we needed the money.

The silent eight stayed silent. Back at the base we prepared for our first task, which was repairing broken stone walls.

'Buckets, sand, crowbars, shovels, hammers,' said Mike.

He only seemed to be able to speak in nouns. We stood around, pretending not to understand. He started to strut like an angry seagull, still not able to get a full sentence out. He decided to lead by example and, left eye twitching, scuttled off to get some tools. The rest of us relented and slowly approached the tool store.

The day had not started promisingly, and things managed to go downhill after we reached the wall, when it became clear that not only did Steve and Mike not have the skills and attributes to work with the long-term unemployed, they knew nothing about building walls. I did know a bit from my time with the British Trust for Conservation Volunteers, but Steve and Mike knew only one thing: that they were in charge and were there to give the orders.

The following week, the IRA bombed the Grand Hotel in Brighton, narrowly missing Margaret Thatcher, but killing and maiming others. During our lunch break, Steve was reading the *Sun*:

'It's a disgrace, a bloody disgrace. We should string the bastards up.'

'I'm just sorry they didn't get Thatcher,' I muttered under my breath, but loud enough for everyone to hear. Steve stalked out of the caravan.

After two more weeks of incompetent leadership, lack of training, the non-appearance of our boots and overalls, and a steady drip of racist, sexist and homophobic comments from the supervisors, I ended up having a flaming row with Mike. After the Thatcher comment, Steve had refused to work with me and Amanda, so we had been put with Mike and one other hapless worker. Some of the work gear had arrived at last, and I was trying to find a pair of overalls that fitted me. I had tried a couple on which, despite being labelled large, came halfway up my calf and were tight round the crotch. I was taking plenty of time. We needed to make up fresh cement for the wall repairs and Andy, the fourth member of our team, was off sick. Mike was quite capable of shovelling some sand into the cement mixer, but he took his role as supervisor very seriously and thought that it was his responsibility to tell us what to do while he watched. Doing a bit of work was clearly beneath his status. He kept coming into the caravan, badgering us to come out and start the mixing. This ended up outside the caravan with me and Mike nose-to-nose while I bellowed in his face: 'If you want some fucking concrete mixed, start fucking mixing it yourself.'

To my surprise, he did just that and kept quiet for the rest of the day, while Amanda and I worked on our stretch of wall. This was the first time I had openly expressed anger at someone else as an adult. I felt a weird mixture of relief that the world hadn't fallen in on me, along with guilt and pleasure at standing up for myself.

Nothing happened for the next six weeks, and then, on Christmas Eve, Amanda's Mum, Mary, saw a man scuttle furtively up to the house, put a letter in the box and rush away. Mike had hand-delivered letters to us both, sacking us with immediate effect. Quite wrongly, Amanda was dismissed by association. In the letter outlining the reasons, I was described as rude, insulting and disruptive of group unity. The first two, *yes*, but only under provocation – but it was Steve and Mike who couldn't unify the group. Amanda and I were about the only two with any social skills in the whole team. The reasons for dismissal also referred to my personal hygiene, and how others didn't want to work with me. This turned out to be the hardcore vegetarian diet-induced flatulence that I suffered from, which only Steve minded. So, I was sacked for farting a lot on an outdoor job: a clear case of discrimination against vegetarians!

Due to being sacked from Fountains Abbey, we had our benefits cut and had to survive for six weeks on less than £15 a week. This contributed to us being stuck in Ripon for three years on the dole, because the initial lack of income and the distress caused by the experience added to the practical difficulties of moving, finding somewhere to live, and securing that elusive, meaningful job. We didn't have a trades union, or anyone to turn to for help in this intensely conservative and forelock-touching part of rural North Yorkshire, but we tried to get the rest of the workers on the scheme to help us get our jobs back and the supervisors disciplined. After some initial promises of sticking with us, the group soon backed down and did nothing. The key rat in this was Ray, who had started on the scheme only two weeks before we were sacked. He had had a brief relationship with Amanda before she went to Bradford, and we thought he was still a friend. He was also educated and articulate and could have swayed the others to support us, which he had promised to do. In fact, he did nothing and three months later, when Mike *was* sacked for serious health and safety lapses, Ray was given his job as supervisor and managed to get a cottage on the estate to boot. No wonder strikers sometimes feel the need to use physical force to keep solidarity intact. The only power we have as ordinary people comes from unity. If we don't stick together, we have nothing.

The following year, I was turned down for another government backed job-creation-scheme job running community sports, for which I was highly qualified through all the coaching I had done at school. I was asked early on at the interview what my political views were (which I refused to answer), and then whether I thought that, as I would be working on a government scheme, I would find my politics compromising. This was clearly illegal and inappropriate.

I wondered what they knew about me and from whom? Another community service job I applied for was to record oral history in Ripon on a scheme that was run by the local teacher-training college. I was the only applicant for the job who met the criteria of having been in receipt of benefit for a year. However, as I was told on the phone, I was turned down because I had a ponytail and a beard. After reaching peak bushiness in Germany, my beard was now trimmed and my hair was neat enough, but they used the excuse that it would frighten the old people.

Although I was determined to dedicate my life to working for peace and justice, this was too nebulous at times to be fully satisfying. I really wanted to make a useful contribution to society. I had done much voluntary work in conservation, but it really wasn't the same as being paid. A pay-packet is a validation of oneself as a person. Loss of self-esteem is a huge issue for people without jobs, and I was no exception.

It wasn't just being unemployed peace and eco-activists that made our everyday lives so different from our fellow townspeople – though our radical politics did make us stick out like clowns at a funeral. There were more personal issues too. Amanda and I both felt constrained by the straitjacket of socially-defined gender roles. Amanda, who by now had cut her long hair short, wore only trousers or shorts, no makeup or bra, only trainers or boots, and didn't remove any body hair. She was rightly furious at the constraints placed on girls and women in our patriarchal society.

I too felt constrained by the pressure to conform to patriarchal gender roles and I wanted to embrace the feminine side of me just as Amanda embraced the masculine in her. I was already taking on and enjoying more domestic responsibilities than most men and I resolved to dress in a more feminine way. I had toyed with cross dressing for several years: not the sexualised sort of transgressive cross-dressing with high heels, stockings, lipstick etc., but androgynous, hippyish and gender-bending cross-dressing. The fact that I was the best part of six-foot-two, broad shouldered and athletic, made it much more difficult to find feminine clothes that fitted me. I simply wanted to express my softer side through clothing. I had a stroke of luck when a new shop opened in the town. For some reason, the proprietor had stocked a pair of pink tracksuit bottoms in my size; lucky for me, and I suspect lucky for the shopkeeper too as he would have struggled to find another buyer.

One day in April, I made up a complete outfit and plucked up the courage to walk into town. I had the pink tracksuit bottoms on with a fluffy pink and purple jumper my mum had knitted, topped off with a blue cotton scarf with gold squares that I'd bought at a festival. My Green and puritan sensibilities didn't really approve of makeup or jewellery, so it was just the clothes. I had a trimmed beard with long hair in a ponytail.

I walked down the steps to the iron gate and turned up the slight hill into town. I was nervous about presenting myself to the world like this, but happy that I had found the courage to try. As I left the houses behind and came alongside a small row of shops and pubs, there was a toot from a van and then a definite whistle. My rear view had elicited sexual approval! I had mixed feelings about this – it wasn't what I was looking for, and I had been well schooled by Amanda to understand that this kind of unrequested attention was sexist and demeaning for women. On the other hand, as I didn't get the kind of appreciation for my looks and body that I vainly thought I deserved from the women in my life, I couldn't help but see it as a compliment. Luckily for all concerned, the van turned left before it passed me, and the driver didn't have the shock of seeing the beard.

On the home front, I took responsibility for cleaning our rooms and, more arduously, doing our laundry. This entailed using Mary's ancient tub and spin dryer and hanging our clothes out on the line in the back yard. One day, I was scrubbing a pair of Amanda's jeans in the kitchen sink as they were too dirty for the machine. Jack came in with a work mate for coffee and cake, as they were working in the local area. I said hello, and the mate made some surprised comment to see me doing laundry. When I told him that they weren't my jeans but Amanda's, he looked confused. After a pause, he said: 'Well, I suppose there's no point keeping a dog and barking yourself.'

There were, however, some real costs to challenging and changing gender roles. It was no doubt one of the reasons our sex life didn't flourish. By this time in Ripon, we had spent the best part of three years together – for twenty-four hours and seven days a week. Was this over-familiarity the reason why Amanda had instigated a period of no penetrative sex? Or, had she come to believe, like Andrea Dworkin, that the act of penetration is always an act of male violence? Was I too male for her? Or, is it that I wasn't male enough? Had the fact that I had taken on much of the domestic and emotional work in our relationship made me less of a man in her eyes? Was it me, or was it men in general? She couldn't or wouldn't tell me. I was left to tread a minefield of unexploded emotions and the barbed-wire barricades of feminist theory and gender fluidity. I did envy the uncomplicated situation of those stags in Studley Park.

20
The Enemy Within

Our third-floor bedroom looked out over a very busy junction, as the main road from Wensleydale joined the road north to the A1 and the A61 south to Leeds. One morning in October 1984, I got up to peer out of the small window. Coach after coach after coach was coming down to the junction and pulling away through the town to head south. Groggy from sleep, it took me some time to see that the buses were full of boys in blue. It was for the miner's strike. It turned out that Ripon army camp had been taken over by the police so that over 1,000 officers could stay there and be bussed to the Yorkshire coalfields to break the picket lines. Our next campaign had landed right on our doorstep.

My best friend from Oxford, big, blond Sam, had finished his degree and moved up to Leeds with a bunch of fellow anarchists. They were a mix of university, poly and town friends from Oxford, who had been drawn together through an alternative lifestyle. They had formed a street theatre group, Dodo Theatre, and were intent on developing this work in inner-city Leeds.

One Wednesday afternoon after work, I took the bus down from Ripon to Leeds to spend four days working with them. Sam and co. had successfully squatted a condemned terraced house on the Meanwood Road.

I arrived late in the afternoon and, after a meal of the usual vegetarian slop, we sat around drinking cheap cider – strengthened by a splash of vodka from a half bottle that was passed round – and smoked a few joints. I couldn't bear the squalor of the kitchen, so after the drink had run out, I washed-up, mopped the floor and then crashed out in my sleeping bag on the manky carpet in Sam's room.

The inspiration for Dodo Theatre was the intense, spare, charismatic ball of energy that was Badal Sircar. Sam had met Badal in Calcutta during his hippie-trail trip to India, before going to university. Badal was in his early 60s and, over the last fifteen years or so, had been developing a radical new approach to theatre in India.

He called it the Third Theatre, because it was an alternative to both the British colonial theatre that dominated the cities and the traditional theatre that still existed in rural areas that was based on the retelling of a small number of stories. These were often conservative in ideology, using costumes, masks and familiar stereotypes.

Badal's idea was to take theatre to people who wouldn't usually go to British style venues, bringing a radical political message to the poor that challenged conservative social norms and ideologies. The Third Theatre would rely on a physical style, performed by a relatively large cast of actors who would help create the pieces through a process of intensive workshopping. Sam successfully bid for some grant money to bring Badal to the UK in the autumn of 1984 for a lecture tour, and so he could also lead some workshops with the newly created Dodo Theatre.

I met Badal the next day in Bradford, where we had secured a free rehearsal space. We started with simple mirroring games, animal impersonations and constructing machines out of people. As the day progressed, Badal increasingly brought in more emotional content. We found ourselves trying to represent starving families in rural India, victims of political torture, peasant farmers, rape victims and the victims of British colonial violence. We became an intertwined mass of writhing and jerking bodies, screaming, shouting and sobbing. Badal was a quietly spoken Indian man of slight physical stature. He smiled a lot and was affable outside of the workshops. Once they got going though, he transformed into a stern and unbending taskmaster. This process of engaging our emotions through repeatedly using our bodies and voices to put ourselves in the shoes of those suffering terrible violence, stripped away our normal defences. After two hours of this process of Badal shouting out details of actual events and real people's suffering, and us trying our best to represent them through our bodies rather than our minds, I was a wreck. Their pain had become visceral, churning up my guts and twisting and tensing my muscles so that I was aching all over. We were left to deal with the emotional cocktail of guilt-by-association – of being White British – and our painful empathy and righteous anger.

At the end of the last day, we went for a celebratory meal at one of Bradford's many curry houses. The staff there were treated to the curious spectacle of a dozen or so young, ragged, white, would-be revolutionaries eating vegetable curries and drinking beer, accompanied by a much older bespectacled Indian man ordering an omelette and a cup of tea, and saying:

'Hot food doesn't agree with me.'

Over the winter, the Dodos continued to meet regularly to work on creating new street theatre pieces. Without Badal's experience and authority, it was difficult to work at the intense level of emotional honesty and engagement that we had managed in his workshops. Without him, we were too conscious of the reactions of others, and some of the group fought against any attempts to show leadership or exert authority. Freeing ourselves to use our bodies to tell stories was challenging for us as untrained actors, and words took over most of the pieces of theatre we were producing.

This process was, however, interrupted by a pantomime for the miners' strike, which *was* script-based (written by Sam and Pete) and very good. We performed the show half a dozen times around Yorkshire in the run up to Christmas and immediately afterwards, livening up some of the parties put on for striking miners and their families by local support groups. It told the story of Super Santa and his helpers (miners) overcoming the wicked witch Scratcher and her sidekicks Pig and the McGrobelly – Ian McGregor, new head of the coal board – monster, by finding a magical piece of coal/kryptonite. As well as the heart-warming victory of good over evil, we had all the traditional elements of slapstick, audience singalong and sweets thrown to the audience. The costumes were good, especially Pig's giant papier-mâché head. Mine, for the McGrobelly monster, included a painted rubber mask, a fearsome dragon-like body, and evil talons attached to painted rubber gloves. My face and hands stank for weeks due to the sweaty rubber. Sexy.

After Christmas, we were asked to do a mini-tour of South Wales, and readily agreed. Our van was a basic Ford Transit, which for some reason was painted a rather unpleasant shade of yellow that bravely displayed the dents and scratches of years' of active service. Few of us could drive, so the cab was appropriated by the two who could, plus Mel (cropped red hair, gay and pregnant under her Dennis the Menace top). We did have blankets and cushions to help with comfort on the floor, but it wasn't my transport of choice for travelling from Leeds to the coal mining valleys of South Wales.

We did our best to get comfortable in the back of the cold, diesel-impregnated van, with some managing to sleep fitfully. Sometime mid-morning, we got hungry. One of our musician friends pulled a large plastic tub out of his bag, and with visible pride said: 'I spent yesterday making this hummus; it's really popular in our house.'

We had the sophisticated accompaniments of crisps and sliced bread. Anyway, we were all hungry and tucked in with gusto. Within minutes, the back of the van smelt worse than the Paris Metro at the end of a long day. Any vampires in the vicinity would have keeled over immediately as the unmistakable stench of garlic filled the poorly-ventilated space. We were somewhere in the Midlands and the smell stayed with us all the way over the Severn Bridge.

When we reached the valleys, the relative smoothness of the motorway was replaced by twisting roads and the frequent stopping and starting at junctions. We had spent seven hours in the back of the van, inhaling the mixed scent of diesel and garlic, and now we were being thrown around all over the floor. Apart from the time when I'd caught dysentery at the Green Gathering, I'd never felt so nauseous in my life. When we finally came to a halt and were let out – blinking and retching into the dark, barren landscape of a pit village – I vowed never to eat hummus again in my life. I would like to have vowed never to travel in the back of a Transit van for eight hours, but I had to face the journey home.

One afternoon, we were going to perform a matinee at Maerdy, one of the bigger pit villages in the area. We arrived and tumbled out of the van to be greeted by a deserted main drag. If there had been a horse, you could have called it a one-horse town.

We found the social club building, one of the biggest on the street, and hauled our gear through the dirty glass doors. The noise hit us like a slap in the face. That was why the village was deserted – everyone was here. It was only three o'clock in the afternoon, but they must have been here for some time. The mood ranged from indifferent to hostile. Several people just walked away when we tried to introduce ourselves, and it took some time before a harassed union official came forward to greet us and show us into his office to use as a changing room. We changed, got set up, were introduced by the same official, and launched into the pantomime. The adults had gathered away from the stage round the side and back of the hall near the bar, and didn't appear to be interested in our show as they carried on talking and drinking. The children were crowded ten to fifteen-deep in front of the stage. We struggled to make ourselves heard. As usual, we encouraged the audience to cheer the heroes and boo the baddies. By our third appearance on stage, however, the crowd had turned ugly and, along with the 'boos', there were shouts to 'fuck off'. Furthermore, we were greeted with a hail of empty drinks containers. (*Exit stage left, pursued by bottles.*) We hurried on until the end whilst dodging missiles, and gratefully sought the sanctuary of our temporary dressing room. We changed as fast as we could, piled back into the van, and got the hell out of there.

It might have been something to do with the fact that Maerdy was the last pit to go back to work at the end of the strike. Out of over 700 miners, not a single man broke rank early. They marched back to work with brass bands and banners flying, defiant to the last. Maybe they were just so tough and self-contained that they didn't need or want us. Luckily, the following show, which took place in a much smaller village in the next valley, was much better received and we headed back to Leeds in reasonable spirits.

Back in Ripon, Amanda and I had set up a support group for the miners' strike. Some of the students from the local college came on board with us, as did some local Labour Party stalwarts. To begin with, it was an exciting and invigorating time. We organised successful fundraising events, like jumble sales and music evenings, but also got people involved and created a positive atmosphere of political opposition in what was, after all, a small and very conservative market town. We were supporting a small village in North Yorkshire whose men worked in the huge Kellingly pit (Super K). This was one of the largest and most modern pits in the country. As the weather got colder, the people were suffering. Most of the families relied on coal for heating, as they normally had plentiful free supplies. Now they needed something else to burn. Amanda and I and one of the students, Jo, roamed the riverbanks and accessible woods and copses around our town to gather free firewood. We packed as much as we could into Jo's VW campervan and drove it down the A1. This used a lot of energy to produce a relatively small amount of heating, but it was a cold winter and the strikers and their families were getting desperate, burning furniture and fittings in their houses. We raised money for food and put on consciousness-raising events, showing films and getting guest speakers.

Amanda and I pledged a regular amount for the fund each week from our very small income. Amanda's mum, Mary, was our most generous supporter. As the Thatcher government became more extreme, she had gradually turned from working-class Tory to leftie-sympathiser.

Amanda and I worked well together as organisers, and we unconsciously developed a slick process for the many events we organised in Ripon for the miners' support group, the peace group, Oxfam Hungry for Change and Amnesty International. It went something like this: as appropriate, book the band, speakers or resources; find and book the venue; make the poster (either hand-drawn or letter-set) and get it printed; take them round the shops and get them displayed in windows; write and send press releases to the two local papers; go around and see the other people we think will support the event to get them on board; ring round other contacts we knew less well; go to meetings to publicise the event.

The first big event to raise funds for the striking miners was a jumble sale to be held on Saturday, 19 January 1985. This was organised under the auspices of the local Labour Party and the poster didn't mention the miners' strike at all, in order not to put locals off. It's hard to imagine now, but before charity shops had taken over most small market towns in England, jumble sales were an important part of local life.

It was easy enough to get donations of clothes and bric-a-brac from an appeal in the local paper. This led to a stream of phone calls, bin bags full of stuff arriving at the house, and a number of journeys on foot around the town to collect bags from people who didn't have a car. Luckily, Amanda's parents had a dining room that was never used, in which we could stack the growing mountain of old clothes.

Our faithful friend Mark, who had moved us from Bradford to Ripon the year before, agreed to take everything down to the YMCA hall in his truck first thing on the morning of the sale. Punters were queuing from 9.30 am for a 10.30 start. We luckily had an ex-headmaster, who was the only Labour councillor in town, to put on the door and keep order. Inside it was mayhem, as we lugged trestle tables around and opened all the bags and tried to find somewhere to display the contents. We formed a rectangular 'wagon circle' with the sellers inside, protected from the hordes by the tables. I gave our team a fierce pep talk:

'We are here to raise as much money as we can for the miners' families to buy food and pay their bills. We will make most of our money in the first half-hour from the best stuff being sold. Stay strong and firm and don't get beaten down. Charge a pound or fifty pence and stick to your guns. We will wait until the last hour to reduce prices.'

The adrenaline kicked in as the doors opened at 10.30, producing a flood-surge of sharp-elbowed bargain hunters. Straight away we were engaged in vicious hand-to-hand combat.

'How much is this jumper love?'

'Fifty pence.'

'I'll give you twenty pence.'

'No, it's fifty; it's in good nick, worth every penny.'

'Thirty pence then?'

'No, I'm sticking to my guns, it's fifty pence – no reductions until 1 o'clock.'

Then, a sour look followed by the handing over of the hard-won fifty pence piece. We had over two hundred people paying ten pence to come in.

Finally, at two o'clock in the afternoon, we finished. In the end we raised £400, which at that time was a stunning amount.

We also made some street collections in Ripon, which took some guts, as the place was full of police, army families and Conservative voters. We were harassed by the local plods. They insisted on taking our names and addresses on a regular basis, even though they had no right to. We didn't feel confident enough to resist this by fighting for our rights when they got aggressive and threatened to arrest us. I think they kept this information on record, because it was following this that we had our mail tampered with and our telephone tapped. A national discourse emerged during the strike, led by the tabloid press and the Tory government, of the 'enemy within', which suggested that active opponents of the government and their policies were somehow enemies of decent, sensible, normal society. Our post stopped coming on a regular basis and would arrive in large quantities, ripped and damaged and roughly repaired with tape. We were being shown that the authorities were looking at our mail. Amanda's Dad, Jack, was a telephone engineer, and he confirmed our suspicions that the odd clicks, absence of ringtones, other calls on the line and being cut off, meant that our phone was being tapped. We weren't so different from Eastern Europe after all, I thought, though thankfully different enough for us not to be sent to prison or worse.

After losing the Fountains Abbey job and failing to get other work and somewhere of our own to live, I was starting to feel more and more cut off from mainstream society. The raw class war of the miners' strike exacerbated the feeling of 'them and us'. We were being cast as the enemy within. Worse than that, us peace activists, anarchists, feminists and greens were only on the fringes of the 'us' that was the industrial working-class that the miners belonged to. We wanted to be part of a wider coalition of opposition with them, but many of those people were put off either by our education, our lack of jobs, our appearance, sexuality, feminist ideas and concern for the environment.

This was brought home to me when the men from the village we had been supporting went back to work, two weeks before the official end of the strike. The people we had been working with down there were so ashamed that they never wanted to talk to us again – despite the sacrifices we had made to help them.

This is another lesson that I learnt through these years of struggle. Most people are only radicalised into action when they are faced with a direct threat. We make it easy for those in power to divide and rule, because most of the time most people will keep their heads down if the threat is against someone else, hoping things will be all right for them.

The effects of losing the strike on me and my friends and associates was to push us further into opposition against not only the state, but many middle-class and conservative working-class people who seemed to be supporting Thatcher and her policies. We were without jobs, without decent housing, and we had experienced the power and force of the state directed against us.

21
Bender in a Bender and Tarzan's Fence

S upporting the miners hadn't stopped our peace activities, and we were still working hard on local campaigns. One weekend in late January 1985 proved particularly memorable.

Peace Members Join Camp

Despite temperatures well below freezing and driving snow, seven members of Ripon for Peace spent an enjoyable weekend at Menwith Hill peace camp. This was the first visit of a series of intended visits by Ripon people to support the camp outside the American base. The camp, which has been in existence since last summer, is the latest in a succession of actions taken by Yorkshire peace groups to try to publicise the existence of the communications base. The next meeting of Ripon for Peace is on February 14th. (The *Ripon Observer* January 31st, 1985.)

I was proud that my work in early 1983, getting Yorkshire peace activists together, was still having ripple effects as local groups continued to set up weekend peace camps at Menwith Hill two years later. Since the summer of 1984, a small group of people had set up a permanent camp, so we were going to support them and boost their numbers and morale for the weekend. The establishment of the permanent camp meant braving the winter in an exposed spot, high up in the Yorkshire Dales.

The older members of Ripon for Peace decided, quite sensibly, to offer their support by driving us to the camp and back and supplying victuals for the weekend. The seven of us mentioned in the local paper included me and Amanda, along with three students from Ripon College, a young newspaper reporter and a teacher. When we arrived at the camp just before seven, the dark was all-enveloping with no streetlights for miles around and, as yet, no visible moon. It was also goolie-witheringly cold.

The camp consisted of a large bender tent, a smaller one, a caravan and a handful of regular two-person tents. The snow, which had been falling for a week or so, was about a foot deep where it lay, soft and undisturbed, whilst amongst the tents it had been compacted to a hard and icy four inches. Wooden pallets and duck-boarding had been laid down to combat the mud during the wet autumn, and these connected the main dwellings.

We were greeted by the five permanent campers, like the soldiers in Mafeking welcoming General Roberts. We dumped our bags in the caravan and quickly piled into the large bender. There was just room for the twelve of us to sit round in a tight circle. To enter, you had to take off your shoes and boots and leave them in a pile in the porch. You then ducked down, opened the blanket-door and crawled into the main dome. The campers had constructed a wood-burning stove out of an old milk churn, and it was already giving off pleasant warmth. Light was provided by a wheezy and ineffective hurricane lamp. One of the older members of Ripon for Peace was particularly friendly with our young journalist and had given him two boxes of goodies to see us through the weekend. Our generous provider, whom we discovered later was struggling with alcoholism and a violent husband (also a pillar of the peace group), had given us three bottles of vodka.

After we had devoured a great pile of food, there was much rummaging around for cups, mugs and beakers. Enough were found and shared out. I had my own trusty tin cup, veteran of many camping expeditions. Then the vodka was passed round. It was dark and consequently difficult to see how much of the clear liquid was slopping into the mugs, so we all ended up with generous measures. The clear spirit was a welcome companion for this cold, dark and essentially futile vigil against imperialist war-mongering. Cocooned in the womblike structure against the harshness of the North Yorkshire winter and the spiritual winter of impending nuclear Armageddon, we thawed out. We chatted, we sang, we got warm and we got merry.

I can't remember who cracked first, we all had young bladders, but in the end it could be put off no longer. We had to take it in turns to crawl out of the circle through the door flap and then into the porch. By the time I got to go, the shoe pile looked like the remnants of a frenetic jumble sale. It was dark, I was pissed as a fart, and I was lucky to even find one of my shoes. I couldn't hold everybody up, so I put on the one shoe and hopped out of the shelter.

I rose to my full six-foot-two-inches tall, stood briefly on one leg, and fell over backwards. I lay on the hard-packed snow looking up at the most intense starlit sky I'd ever seen. I roared with laughter. Thanks to the many layers of clothes and the vodka, I felt no pain at all. I rolled onto my side, pushed myself up onto my knees, and managed to get up again. I hopped a few yards further on and, whoops, I fell again. I lay there longer, entranced by the stars. Common sense kicked in and I sacrificed a leg warmer by putting it over my shoeless foot and walked more securely out of the camp and over the road to piss in the copse of scrub and small trees outside the base. The problem with wearing so many layers of clothing was how difficult it made getting my now shrunken member out from the depths of trousers, tracksuits and long-johns. The women had a different problem. They had to drop their trousers and squat in the freezing cold. Three of them decided to walk as short a distance as possible from the camp, so didn't cross the road. They were in a line when a rare car whooshed past. They were lit up in the full beam of the headlights like characters in an avant-garde cabaret.

It was bedtime and Amanda and I had agreed to sleep in the caravan, as it had a double bed and we were the only couple. A caravan is of course only a tin box on wheels, and the coldest of all the accommodation on offer. We kept all our clothes on, got into our sleeping bags, put our coats on top and slipped our hats and gloves back on. In the morning, as I looked up at the thick ice on the inside the caravan, I was seriously worried about the risk we had run of getting hypothermia. The following night there was no vodka and we found extra blankets to help, but it was still ferociously cold in the early hours of the morning, as I lay awake with anxious thoughts about my future.

Our little camp in the Yorkshire Dales merited a few lines in the local newspapers. Events at the Molesworth Cruise Missile site were, however, gaining national attention. The government was determined to take on and defeat their so-called 'enemy within'. They had gained confidence with the success of the aggressive policing of the miners' strike and were now looking to demonstrate the power of the state to all other dissidents.

The eviction of around a hundred people who were living on the base happened on 6 February when 1,500 troops and police were deployed to secure the seven-mile station perimeter. The troops had been training for weeks for the rapid deployment of a three-metre-high wire fence, behind which a five-metres-wide no-man's land concrete roadway was constructed. Finally, another three-metre-high fence, this time steel, was erected beyond that. Floodlights were installed every hundred yards and Ministry of Defence Police and armed guards patrolled the fence twenty-four hours a day. The cost of the operation to clear and fence the base at Molesworth was in the order of £6.5 million. Minister for Defence, Michael 'Tarzan' Heseltine, rocked up in a flak-jacket and posed proudly for photos as his mane of golden hair fluttered in the wind.

We took a minibus down on the Saturday to show solidarity and support for the remaining peace campers. We returned to Ripon slightly shaken by the roadblocks, barbed wire and large numbers of police, helicopters and watchtowers. This show of strength from the government was responded to by national CND, who had already agreed to focus on Molesworth for a national demonstration at Easter 1985, but who now also started to plan a mass blockade of the base for February 1986.

The defeat of the miners' strike and the hard line taken by the authorities at Molesworth were dispiriting, but it made me more determined than ever to do whatever I could to achieve disarmament. The first nine months of 1985 became an intense and frenetic period of activism. I threw absolutely everything I had left into the struggle.

22
These Boots Were Made for Walking

After our chastening visit to the now heavily-defended Molesworth, in March Amanda and I decided to join a peace walk from Sizewell (the site of a Nuclear Power station on the Suffolk coast) to Molesworth. It was due to arrive in time for the national demonstration in April. Our lorry-driving friend Mark dropped us off at the end of the Doncaster by-pass and we hitched a lift. We waited about twenty minutes and then got picked up by a Slumberland wagon and its cheerful cockney driver Mick from Elephant and Castle. We had a good natter about all sorts of things, including his feelings about television killing the brain and ruining social events. We were left on a lay-by on the A604 that was again cold and windy – now with a hint of hail. After a couple of minutes of hitching, a car with CND stickers stopped. The driver was, unusually, a woman, an ex-social worker now a lecturer, on her way to Cambridge. She told us about going on the Aldermaston marches as a student, and then dropped us off at the junction with the A45. Now it was really hailing. We had to wait about half an hour and then got picked up by another lorry. The driver opined that people were too sensible to have a nuclear war, and that the amount spent on so-called defence was criminal. He was also against the Sizewell nuclear power station and didn't like the US servicemen who were all over the area. He dropped us off at Stowmarket on the turnoff to Yoxford in East Suffolk. We soon got a lift a few miles up the road from a young chap in a van who sold and installed wood-burning stoves – he had a tweed cap, a luxuriant red beard and a Flann O'Brian novel on the dashboard. The road was looking quiet by then, but it was relaxing to be off the main roads. We waited twenty to thirty minutes and got a short lift with a friendly older man who turned out to be the curator of Saxted Mill, a beautiful, working windmill. Back on the side of the road it was extremely cold and windy, but after a while we crammed into a rickety old mini with an off-duty vicar for the two or so miles to Framlingham. We had a much-needed coffee in the marketplace and walked back out to find a very quiet road. A few posh cars swished by and things weren't looking good. Being in a couple generally helped us get lifts, but we were scruffy long-hairs carrying two big rucksacks.

After what felt like an eternity, a fruit-and-veg lorry appeared, and I pleaded with the driver with my eyes. He stopped – thank you Hitchhiking Gods – and we talked about bananas all the way to Saxmunden. We finally arrived at our destination, the signal box on the railway at Leiston, at about six o'clock in the evening. We had made it in ten hours with seven lifts. It was my first, and only, visit to a working signal box, which almost made the journey itself worthwhile. It got better, though, as our host for the night was the signalman, Bill Howard, who was a lifelong Communist. He regaled us with stories of how the left-wing Leiston town council had flown the red flag over the town hall when Stalin joined the war against Hitler. Over a delicious fish-and-chip tea with his family, we talked more about the new Sizewell B reactor. Bill had presented evidence to the official enquiry from a poll in which a third of local people had voted and, of those, three quarters were against Sizewell B. He talked of the deaths of workers that went unreported and the private detectives sent to investigate all the people who had objected at the enquiry.

In the morning, we walked the two hundred yards to the beach at Sizewell, which was dominated by the bleak square of the nuclear power station. Our fellow peace marchers arrived in dribs and drabs throughout the day. After a brisk walk on the beach in the usual stiff easterly wind, we mostly spent our time in the double-decker bus that was to be the march's support vehicle. After dark we gathered in a barn close to the power station. It was a modern barn with a clean but rough concrete floor, corrugated iron walls, and it was to be our home for the night. About forty of us sat in a large circle, on straw bales or old chairs, in candlelight supplemented with a few dim electric lamps. It was cold and we had endured a long day without much to do.

The march had been organised by a capable and jolly middle-aged couple who lived locally on a smallholding. They suggested that we should go round the circle one at a time saying why we were committing ourselves to this march. People spoke simply, directly and from the heart. The effect of hearing people's genuine horror at the way the world was going and their sincere wishes to be active in creating a better one, was electrifying. Our words rang out in the softly-lit silence.

'I've come on this peace march because it's the Easter holidays and I'm a teacher. I want the seven-year-olds I teach, and all the seven-year-olds in the world, to grow up without having to fear nuclear war.'

'We live just down the road from here and we want to stop people living with the risk of accidents or attacks or natural disasters causing nuclear contamination. Nuclear weapons need the by-products of nuclear power and we want to stop both.'

'I've been actively opposing nuclear weapons for five years now. In that time more and more are being made. There are enough nuclear weapons in the world to destroy it several times over, if that's even possible. We've just got to stop this madness. So, I feel I've got to keep on protesting until we get disarmament.' (This last one was me.)

'Cruise missiles are evil. They're part of this sickening first strike policy that Reagan and his cronies think could win a nuclear war. I really admire what the women have done at Greenham; I thought it was about time I did something too.'

'I'm a Buddhist and we believe that killing is wrong. I've also had the chance to visit Hiroshima. We mustn't let that happen again, ever.'

'I've been on a few of the big CND demos in London and I've paid my subs to CND for a few years and worn the badge. I saw this march advertised, and I thought: You can do this Steve, you're between jobs, and you've always said you wanted to do more. So here I am.'

'I'm a Quaker from Cambridge and we support many peace initiatives in my meeting. This march is happening in our neck of the woods and I wanted to show the other older members of the meeting that it is never too late to really speak "Truth to Power".'

'I don't want to live in a world where so-called peace is thought to be best achieved by threatening death on an unimaginable scale.'

'I'm a Christian. Jesus said, love thy enemy. You can't love someone if you're threatening to kill them.'

'This is too important to leave it to the politicians and generals. It's our world, our future, and ordinary people have to stand up for what is right.'

We gained enormous strength from hearing each other's stories and voices. The public discourse around the peace movement was full of sneering about misguided and well-intentioned woolly liberals, stooges of the Soviets and overemotional women. But to hear, and *really listen to*, so many people willing to stand up publicly for what they believed in was both humbling and inspiring. We had unleashed some of that hidden power that comes from honesty, openness and righteousness.

Amanda and I started the peace march the next day on the Suffolk coast, but after a week we had to be rescued by my Dad after a bad bout of the runs. He drove up from Chelmsford to Suffolk to take us back home to recover. He also caved in to pressure and drove us back to Cambridge a few days later to rejoin the peace march. Mum came too, and as we drove up the M11 the silence was broken by Dad who had been reading the *Daily Telegraph* that morning:

'The Soviets have far more tanks than us and if they decide to invade Western Europe, we don't have the conventional forces to stop them, so we need a nuclear deterrent.'

I was always ready to debate about disarmament, as my time in Bradford had given me a very good grasp of the facts and figures as well as the main arguments. I explained that the Russians did have more tanks than us, but that most of them were from the Second World War and many probably didn't work. I went on to say that these tanks were much more useful for intimidating the civilian population of Eastern Europe than launching an invasion of the West. Dad wasn't convinced, so I went on to ask: 'What you think is the best way of stopping a tank?'

'Other tanks – like at El Alamein,' Dad replied.

I brought up the fact that the West had vastly superior anti-tank missiles, both ground-and air-launched. Technology is what the West was good at and we could destroy the Soviet tanks in a day if they started amassing near the border.

'I'll have to take your word for that,' said Dad.

Mum, looking for a way to keep the peace, offered mint humbugs all round.

'Surely the whole point of these nuclear weapons is to stop us being attacked by threatening Mutually Assured Destruction?' Dad re-started the argument.

I was able to quote a string of figures, explaining how the West had developed and used nuclear weapons first, at the end of the War, and had superiority over the Soviets until much later, when the USSR acquired the delivery capacity to launch a devastating attack on us too. In contrast, we had enough warheads by 1954 to destroy the whole of the Soviet Union and much more. Dad then brought up the Cuban missile crisis as an example of Mutually Assured Destruction in action and I told him that we were much closer to a nuclear war than people realised at the time. I was getting worked up and raised my voice to say: 'If we accept Mutually Assured Destruction has worked for twenty-five years, why do we keep building more and more nuclear weapons?'

'We have to keep up with the Russians of course.'

'No, we only need enough bombs to destroy them once – there's no point in bombing the rubble into smaller rubble.'

'Well, you just can't trust them. Look, it was only a few years ago that they invaded Afghanistan and they're still fighting there.'

'You're changing the subject, you always do that when we argue,' I snapped.

Mum spoke up from the back, pointing out a bird of prey hovering over the carriageway. Looking over my shoulder I could see Amanda smirk at this obvious ploy to diffuse the tension. It only worked temporarily as Dad had his dander up too: 'The Russians won't be satisfied until they've taken over the whole world with their foul ideology. We must be strong enough to stop them. You might want to live in a workers' paradise where you have to queue for bread and can get locked up for saying boo to a Party member, but I certainly don't.'

I took a deep breath and let some time pass before I brought the subject back to nuclear strategy. I said that if the threat of Mutually Assured Destruction had been so successful, it was strange that we were risking this by allowing Cruise missiles to be stationed in Britain. I explained that the peace movement was so against Cruise because the Americans claimed that they were first-strike nuclear weapons. They, along with Reagan's 'Star Wars' plans for missile defence systems, were part of a strategy to win a nuclear war.

'Win a nuclear war! That's ridiculous, I can see why you're against that,' Dad said.

It seemed that, for the first time, he had been persuaded by the logic of my arguments. This new understanding disappeared by the next time we saw each other. I learnt the hard way that arguing with people on issues of peace and war and disarmament was never really about facts and figures. History, statistics and logical arguments were all very well, but as always with political debate, people – including me of course – squeeze facts to fit in with their existing belief systems.

Amanda and I were recovered enough to join the marchers in Cambridge for the last leg to Molesworth and then on to the national demonstration. The main march was routed around as much of the perimeter of the airbase as was possible. We were in the region of 10,000 souls who this Easter had come to continue the protest against the siting of cruise missiles at Molesworth. I had hoped to see ten times that number. Were people getting demo-weary? I wondered. As the protest snaked around the muddy tracks near the fence on one side of the base, we were spread out, no more than three or four abreast.

I don't know why the skips were there, but they were just what the young, self-styled black-clad anarchists needed. There were around sixty of them and they were having a fine old time. The noise grew louder as we approached. Some of them were using wooden stakes to drum violently against the metal sides. A fire had been lit in one of the skips and licks of flames were shrouded by billowing black smoke as the rubbish burned. Chants of 'Maggie Thatcher's boot boys' rose and fell on the breeze along with individual cries of 'smash the state', 'class war', and 'kill the pigs'. We were about 200 yards away when a volley of bricks and stones and rubble was hurled at the police, who were grouped in front of the fence. The police had to use shields and nimble footwork to avoid the accurate missiles. The anarchists must have built up a good supply of ammo as a more considered bombardment followed the initial volley.

The mostly middle-aged, middle-class peace protesters filed past this outbreak of anger and violence. This was the first time I had seen violence on a peace demonstration in Britain. Had it been two or three years previously, the protesters and stewards would have stepped in to stop it. However, it now felt like we were losing the chance to persuade our government to take disarmament seriously. The miners' strike had been defeated, and the police appeared to have been enthusiastic participants in going way beyond their legal remit to ensure victory for the government. The Convoy had also been beaten up in the so-called 'Battle of the Beanfield' by the boys in blue, and the peace camps and Rainbow camp at Molesworth had been recently evicted with a show of strength from the army and police. So, ordinary peace activists felt much more anger towards the police than had been the case a few years before. Although most people on the demo would never have dreamt of throwing things themselves, they understood the young people's anger and, on one level, thought the police deserved what they were getting. Part of me thought that too, but more than anything I still wanted the peace movement to be successful, and I firmly believed that non-violence was a key part of our strength.

Rather than keep with the main route of the march, I cut across the no-man's-land between the demonstrators and the base and stood still between the police and the anarchists. Amanda immediately realised what I was doing and joined me. We stood together holding hands, facing the rock throwers. I was prepared to dodge oncoming missiles but, to be fair to the anarchists, they stopped straight away. We stood alone, and time appeared to stand still. My heart was thumping wildly in my chest and I gripped Amanda's hand firmly. We didn't look at each other, but both stared straight ahead. No one else from the march joined us. The police behind us said nothing, and the anarchists didn't shout abuse at us.

This is the heart of the experience of non-violent action. We put our bodies in danger to make a moral point. There was no need for words, and it was crystal clear to everyone what we meant and what was happening. Me, in my Casey Jones dungarees, thick woolly jumper, shaggy hair and beard, Amanda in her white-and-rainbow-striped CND bobble hat and her dad's old blue GPO jacket with a web-of-life embroidered on the back.

We stood and waited and eventually re-joined the line of people filing round the base. Several hours later, as we headed away from the base after the rally and speeches, we saw the police form a wedge and make a swift and decisive strike out from their position to grab a handful of the anarchists whom they had identified as ringleaders from the earlier stone-throwing. These young anarchists hadn't yet learned the importance of covering their faces and then melting away, if they were going to throw stuff at the police. They also hadn't learnt another important lesson: don't underestimate the police or other agents of the state. Just because you think they must be dull-witted and incompetent, it doesn't mean they are!

23
Caught Red-Handed

Early in 1985, Amanda and I had hatched a plan with two other young activists for a peace walk from Fylingdales to Menwith Hill, going through much of North Yorkshire, bringing the struggle for peace into the heart of our own conservative communities. Between the four of us, we liaised with all the existing local peace groups, organised the route, accommodation, transport and other practicalities and put together a media action plan.

We started the walk early in August on a Monday. As it did every Monday, the base tested its siren and we pretended to die in a nuclear attack outside the main gate. In the event, it was mostly the local sheep that witnessed this protest, but we had managed to get a journalist from the local paper to come, and he took a good photo showing scattered 'corpses' and officials in radiation suits. On this morning, notable mainly for the torrential rain (I had begun to wonder if God was against us with all this precipitation), thirty of us packed up the camp and walked to Pickering. The first stop was the warm-and-dry Quaker meeting house.

We left Pickering in high spirits to walk to Kirkby Moorside, where there was a small peace group that was keen to get a boost of energy from welcoming us. Our overnight stop was at Howard's – a local activist – field sharing with friendly goats. Oswaldkirk was next along the route and the journey was improved by a country pub that sold chocolate. We camped in Rosemary's back garden (another local activist), and she went beyond the call of duty by allowing extremely grubby peace walkers to use her immaculate bathroom. Howard (of Howard's field) saved the day after the exhaust fell off the lime-green ambulance which was our main luggage transporter. He improvised with a bit of wire to hold the exhaust on and this lasted for the whole trip.

We were heading for Easingwold, which was home to a civil defence college and housed the bunkers to be used by North Yorkshire Council in the event of a nuclear attack. This had been the site of the first Yorkshire-wide NVDA back in 1983 and it was our intention to engage in some renewed direct action there. We gathered in a tight circle on the roadside grass next to our makeshift camp.

Penny and Douglas were the other two young leaders. At eighteen and nineteen, they were younger and much less experienced than us. It was Douglas who spoke first. He was tall, and his slender figure was emphasised by his impossibly skinny jeans. He had wild blond hair dyed with streaks of pink. His brown eyes burned with passion as he said: 'This is our chance to really do something, it's what we've been waiting for. There isn't much security here, so if we are quick, we can get straight in, maybe right inside really do something to let them know we mean business. Who's up for some proper action, maybe painting all over their precious bunker?'

'Yeah,' said Penny, 'I'm tired of just leafleting and doing die-ins and street theatre. If we are going to get this government to listen to us, we need to start doing stuff that gets noticed. The world is getting more dangerous every day and we can't just sit on our bums and do nothing.'

'Yeah, let's do it,' shouted sixteen-year-old Keith.

'Hang on, hang on,' I said, 'before we get carried away, we need to get a consensus from the group about how far we are comfortable taking things. I'm not sure I want to start breaking and entering or

Fig. 14. Leading the N. Yorks peace march

151

chucking paint around. How about if we have a day of nonviolence training tomorrow where we can talk through these issues and prepare ourselves for possible arrest and trial?'

'We can't waste time, if people are up for it, I think we should just do it. If you don't want to get involved, that's fine, but you can't stop us.' Penny said.

'I'm not trying to stop anyone and it's not about me, it's about what the group wants collectively. I've spent the last four years doing direct actions and I've seen how people can rush in and then regret it afterwards,' I replied, trying hard to keep my cool.

'I know I won't regret it,' said Douglas. 'This is what I've been waiting for, the chance to really do something. No one is going to stop me.'

My experience of direct action had left me emotionally scarred, and I was no longer confident that, in a heated situation, I would act in a constructive, non-violent way. I felt strongly that proper preparation was essential.

Penny and Douglas then surrounded themselves with a group who wanted to take immediate and, possibly, extreme action, and cut off communication with the rest of us. The next day, fifteen walkers and local supporters went into the college and painted slogans on the walls of the building. We were made to look like irresponsible idiots in the *Yorkshire Evening Post* in an article that focussed on the fact that a twelve-year-old girl had been involved and that five protesters were caught literally red-handed, hiding in the woods with red paint on their hands that matched the colour of the slogans daubed on the walls. These five were bound over for two years and ordered to pay £30 compensation.

It was a very strange experience to find myself cast in the role of conservative grown-up, urging caution and responsibility. The peace movement in general was made up of middle-aged, middle-class folk with jobs and families. I was usually the young subversive firebrand, coming up against the disapproval of more conventional peace activists. My self-confidence had been undermined over the last few years by people's hostility to, and rejection of, my desire for a peaceful world – and the social rejection of me as a person because I didn't fit into conventional society. I hurt a lot because I hadn't found much support within the wider peace movement from people who were more socially conventional, and I wanted to protect Penny and Douglas from the same fate.

This conflict was, however, symptomatic of wider strains in the peace movement. As we came up against the power of the state and were forced to contemplate failing to achieve our aims, it was harder to maintain solidarity in what was, after all, a diverse movement. In pre-internet days, the main forums for discussion were magazines, *Peace News* for pacifists and non-violent activists, and CND's magazine *Sanity*. During this second half of 1985, I noticed increasing numbers of accusatory letters and articles appearing. People were castigated by small, holier-than-thou groups for not being feminist enough, vegan enough, anarchist enough. Labour activists hit out at those of us who wouldn't work for their party. Greens and anarchists accused Labour of being part of the problem, and of course, the Trotskyists attacked everyone else.

Our march had to go on though, and I had to attend to much of the practical organisation. After leafleting in Thirsk, we walked to Northallerton, the county town of North Yorkshire. The walk there included a drenching in a thunderstorm, but the good people of the local CND group gave us hot baths and took our clothes away to dry. This sort of help was vital to keep body and soul together through this unseasonably bad weather. Northallerton saw the first performance of our street theatre *The Bunker Game*. It was also the stage for an unpleasant, but not uncommon, encounter with a local resident while we were taking a breather *en route* to picketing County Hall:

'Hey, you – yes you there – get off my wall!' said the angry bald man in frayed but immaculately ironed overalls, holding a garden fork.

'What's the matter? We're just having a rest,' I replied.

'It's a garden wall, it's not built for sitting on, you might break it.'

We reluctantly got back to our weary feet.

'What are you doing here anyway?' said the gardener.

'We're walking from Fylingdales to Menwith Hill, on a peace march – would you like one of our leaflets?' I leaned forward and proffered one.

'No, I most certainly would not. I suppose you are happy for the Russians to walk all over us?'

'No, we...'

'You're all young, aren't you? Well I remember the last war and if we hadn't stood up against Hitler, we'd all be speaking German now.'

'Oh, come on, this is different, we're talking about weapons of mass destruction, that would kill us all,' I said, weary of this kind of provocative barb that didn't really want an answer.

'We need to be strong, and disarmament just encourages our enemies,' the man persisted.

'Hello Bill, what's going on?'

'Oh, hello June, this lot were using my wall as a park bench, and I told 'em to get off. They want to ban the bomb.'

The women turned on us immediately: 'You lot are a disgrace... my husband, God help him, was held by the Japs for three years. When he got home, he was a shadow of the man I married. He died two years later. You've got no respect. He served his country and went through hell and you lot want to make friends with the people who did it to him. You make me sick.'

June turned away and marched off, as I said to the back of her beige mac:

'I'm really sorry about your husband, but we want to stop wars, so nobody has to suffer like that.'

'On your way, son, I think we're done here,' said Bill, bending down and ostentatiously checking his roses for damage.

We carried on walking to Ripon (a night in a bed!) and Harrogate. Saturday morning brought another winter's day in summer and we trudged off in the mud and rain to Menwith Hill, our final destination. We were fifty strong by now, and the extra people made it bearable. After we had arrived and all the tents were up, the camp looked superb and I could relax and feel proud of the results of all my efforts. We were joined on Sunday by at least another hundred activists and about fifty took part in a picnic-trespass on the base. We had managed to co-ordinate groups of activists from all over Yorkshire to take part in this Non-Violent Direct Action. We climbed over a gate at the side of the base with food and drink and found a pleasant spot near one of the 'golf-balls' (the covering for the spy-satellites). We started to have a picnic before being unceremoniously dragged out by the MOD police.

During the winter of 1985-6, we continued to concentrate on local activity until CND designated Molesworth as the target for their next nationally-organised NVDA. A complete blockade of the base was planned for 6 February 1986, exactly a year after the high-profile securing of the base in February 1985. This was the first mixed (as opposed to women only) national NVDA since Upper Heyford in 1983, which had been relatively successful and well supported. The imminent arrival of operational cruise missiles and the urgency of this final phase of construction work led us to believe that the authorities would not allow us to close the base down, so we were expecting mass arrests and confrontation.

In Yorkshire the preparation for this action was more comprehensive than for any of the previous ones. A network of non-violence trainers was now well established, and sessions were offered in most of the big cities: Leeds, Bradford, Sheffield, Hull, Wakefield, Huddersfield and York. We organised one for North Yorkshire, in Ripon.

Amanda and I prepared, organised and delivered a day-long workshop to ten participants. In the end, we were part of a nine-strong affinity group which faced another early start, long drive and a day out in very cold wintery conditions. Thousands of activists from around the country came down for the day and the base was effectively sealed off for the demonstration. The authorities decided, to our great surprise, to opt for non-confrontation and allowed us the small victory of stopping construction vehicles for one day. This

Fig, 15. NVDA Training, Menwith Hill

Fig. 16. (top). Climbing in and being dragged out of Menwith Hill

victory had, however, cost the protestors huge resources of time, energy and money.

The fact that after six years of massive mobilisation for peace demonstrations, marches, vigils, petitions, letter-writing, peace camps, die-ins, tree planting, paper-crane making to mark Hiroshima Day, street theatre and the like – all over the country – only

Fig. 17. Unceremonious ejection from Menwith Hill

around 6,000 people were willing to take this kind of direct action, made it clear that it was never going to be more than symbolic. We were never going to get enough people to really shut down a base and cause so much trouble for the authorities that they would either have to use draconian powers against peaceful protestors, or start seriously considering our arguments. Six thousand people willing to take direct action is, on one level, impressive, but without a culture of non-violent resistance taking root across the country, this could never be sustained. I was far from alone in being worn down by years of protesting, and this blockade, big as it was, marked the end of mass mobilisation for NVDA.

What turned out to be my last peace demo for seventeen years was on a much smaller scale. In late April 1986, Mrs Thatcher allowed the US air force to use British bases and airspace to carry out bombing raids over Libya, which unavoidably included civilian targets. I had been bed-ridden with a bad back for at least two weeks at the time of the bombing. I had been two-thirds of the way through decorating our bedroom when the pain came on. As part of our attempt to reconnect with the mainstream, Amanda had taken a job at a garden centre at nearby Boroughbridge. Amanda would go to work all day and return bad-tempered and unsympathetic. I was in pain, bored and angry with her. We weren't having much of a sex life – not just because of the bad back – and I was extremely frustrated, personally and politically.

Like many others in the peace movement, I was despairing at our lack of success over the last seven years, the seemingly impregnable Tory hegemony and the rise of the 1980s' 'greed is good' yuppie culture. This latest horror of allowing our country to be the launchpad for the bombing of civilians was a flagrant abuse of British sovereignty and international law and was the last straw for many of us. We had to protest about it, but without any hope of being listened to.

To our credit, in Ripon – this small conservative market town in North Yorkshire – around twenty people gathered in the marketplace for a spontaneous demonstration against the outrage on the evening the news came out. I got out of bed and walked very slowly and in considerable pain up into town to be part of this show of disapproval. I felt proud of this bunch of ordinary people, determined to say publicly: Not in our name. But I felt inconsolably desolate at the knowledge that it would make absolutely no difference and that the great cause I'd sacrificed so much for seemed to have come to nothing. I shuffled home, staring at the pavement, in intense physical and emotional pain.

24
From Street Theatre to Terrorism

Emboldened by their crushing victory in the 1983 General Election, the Conservative government pushed ahead with its neo-liberal economic revolution. The population was to be bribed with cheap shares and cheap council houses. Trades unions were to be disciplined with stringent anti-union laws and workers kept in their place through record unemployment levels. The rich were to get richer via owning newly privatised industries, and the poor were to suffer poverty, social exclusion and blame for their own misfortune. Political enemies and social deviants were to be dealt with harshly. The Cold War was still hot, and environmental disasters made the headlines. This was the backdrop to my increasingly desperate attempts to change the world in the mid-1980s.

After the rollercoaster ride of the Dodo Theatre pantomime tour and its failure to win the strike for the miners, Sam bought an old single-decker bus and the group started to prepare for our next project. We wanted to take theatre to the working-class communities of the North of England. Living together on the bus, we would find somewhere to park up for the night and in the morning go into a nearby town. We searched for wide streets, public squares or green spaces near the central shopping area where we could perform our plays to the passing crowds. During the month that I was on board in the summer of 1985, there were plenty of days when we were either moved on by police or private security in shopping malls, or it rained too hard to be worth performing – or, worst of all, we performed to monumental indifference. However, there were also days when we gathered decent-sized audiences and received a positive response.

The first time I experienced this was in Nelson in East Lancashire. We came into the square off the main shopping street at about eleven o'clock in the morning, banging our drums and then launched into our strongest play in terms of visual impact and noise—*The Oppressed Person*. By the time we had finished, a large crowd had gathered to watch. We gave them our most successful piece, *The Exploitation Game*.

159

I didn't perform in this play and so I busied myself giving out leaflets. At its peak, our audience numbered around 120, and people laughed at the jokes and cheered when one family rejected crass consumerism for authentic experience. At that time, we only had four finished plays, so we did the other two – one about the iniquity of our prison system and one lampooning the promotion of romantic love as the solution to all of life's ills. We took a half-hour break and did them all over again. This reception and genuine engagement with our work boosted our shaky confidence and morale. This was the real thing. We were cultural revolutionaries smashing down the false constructs of the dominant ideology, encouraging resistance and revolution amongst the oppressed and poverty-stricken victims of Thatcherism and post-industrial decline. In the evening, I cooked dinner over an open fire, and we sat around talking excitedly and singing revolutionary songs late into the night.

A few days later I had to return to Ripon to sign on and, as usual, chose to hitchhike to save money. I signed on and was on the journey back when I got a lift just outside Harrogate. The driver was a thick-set man in his forties with long curly black hair. We set off accompanied by the throaty roar of a powerful Ford Granada and were soon cruising at seventy miles an hour.

We chatted amiably enough, but then came the thorny question from my driver: 'So, what you do for a living?'

I've never been quick enough to lie convincingly in this situation, so I replied: 'I'm unemployed at the moment.'

'Well stay with me. I can give you a job.'

'Really?'

'Yeah, I'm a site foreman in North Wales and I'm on my way back there now. We're short of blokes to do the labouring at the moment – you look fit enough.'

'Erm…' – panicking and playing for time – 'I don't have anything with me, no change of clothes, no toothbrush, nothing.'

'I could get you kitted out with work clothes and boots, and you can easily buy a toothbrush. It's cash-in-hand, decent money.'

I felt awful refusing this kind offer. I could just hear this thoroughly decent bloke telling his mates: 'Well, half of these buggers don't even want to work. Last week I had this young bloke in the car – he was hitching, and I gave him a lift – he said he was out of work, so I offered him a start on the spot, and he turned me down flat, lazy sod…'

As I got out near Blackburn, he asked again: 'Sure you don't want to change your mind?'

'Thanks, but no thanks; I've got people expecting me here.'

'Suit yourself.'

The bus was still where I had left it, and although most of the group were out performing, a couple had stayed behind to mind the camp.

'All right Chris?' asked Pete.

'Yeah, thanks, but a bit shocked – I've just been offered a job on a building site in North Wales.'

'Jesus, you've had a narrow escape.'

'Yeah, it was really weird saying no.'

'I know what you mean, but Wales, eh?'

'I thought he might kidnap me anyway and I'd be stuck on some godforsaken mountainside, carrying buckets of cement all my life. The money would be nice, and it would be good to be able to say for a change that I was working for a living. He seemed like a decent bloke too, but I just don't think I could have done it. I've never worked on a building site and the other guys might not have accepted me.'

'I'm glad you're back though mate – no one else cooks half as well as you,' said Pete.

That cheered me up no end and I had a roll-up and made some tea.

During this period, the Great Gob himself, Bob Geldof, launched Band Aid. In response to images of starving Africans, British people enjoyed a megastar rock concert and gave some money for food aid. I'm proud to say that as far as I know, we were the only people in the country who actually protested against this celebrity love-in, that in our opinion would do nothing to really help the situation in Africa. Where the organisers saw bands using their popularity to raise money to aid the starving, we saw misguided liberals or shallow opportunists sticking a *band-aid* on the deep and festering wounds that the Western powers had inflicted on Africa through slavery, colonisation and proxy wars. This illustrates clearly how far we had moved from mainstream society and how angry and alienated we felt. Whilst the nation basked in self-congratulation, we gave out embittered leaflets in the rain to unemployed young people in the decaying industrial towns of East Lancashire.

Our analysis was that the ordinary people of Britain had in fact got common cause with the ordinary people of Africa. We were all pawns in the hands of the rich and powerful. I was rejecting the possible wealth and status on offer in our society, in solidarity, in part at least, with the poor people of the world. I certainly did not think that it was right for Westerners to live in such comparative luxury whilst most humans struggled to subsist. Living on sub-benefit levels of income for seven years was my way of standing in solidarity with the poor around the world. It was also, in part, an act of penitence for the past colonial and racist sins of my country.

Towards the end of my time on the bus, we endured an enforced lay-up due to mechanical failure. We were stranded halfway between Bolton and Wigan on the crest of the scarily-named Hunger Hill, waiting for a new gearbox. This situation seemed to be an apt metaphor for my own life. I had reached an impasse, not able to move on, but not liking where I was. Over the last four years I had left my old world – my roots – completely behind. Chelmsford Chris, Head Boy Chris, Captain Chris, prize-winning Chris, Oxford student Chris, normal, short-haired Chris, were all a distant memory. So, sadly, was the optimistic peace activist Chris, who thought that the world really was going to change through non-violent direct action.

In the four years since I had left Oxford to work for a peaceful, equal and green utopia, I had gone from having the world at my feet to having the world on my case. I had been harassed, assaulted and arrested by the police and my post had been opened and my phone tapped. I had had bottles, shit, spit and insults hurled at me by those who didn't like talk of peace. I had been sacked from work and then denied jobs because of my appearance and political views, and I had no chance of getting decent housing. More hurtful to me than the direct attacks, were the subtle barbs from some middle-class peace activists. As the peace movement began to realise that it was not going to be successful, people began to turn on each other. People with careers and houses and families sometimes felt threatened by my level of activism and commitment as it made their own efforts seem small. Sometimes they just didn't approve of alternative lifestyles. People at local group meetings directed comments to me like:

'It's all right for you, you don't have a mortgage to pay.'

'The public are put off by scruffy peace activists on the dole.'

'Are you really trying to get a job?'

These attacks from my own side added to my sense of social disapproval and hastened the seeping away of my self-esteem and self-confidence. The whole world seemed to be against me and my mates, and that was a crushing weight to bear. The trouble was that, in return, we were turning against the whole world too. Everybody hated us so we started to hate everybody back.

A couple of months before the street theatre tour, Sam and I had daubed the wall of a supermarket with two-metre high letters: 'EAT SLEEP WORK CONSUME DIE'. We were railing against what we saw as the ability of people with money and power to be able to keep the majority of the population helpless in the glare of television-fuelled, mindless consumption. What would it take for people to wake up to what was going on around them? Was four million unemployed not enough? How about millions of starving children in Africa? Perhaps the threat of nuclear holocaust might do the trick? What about the prospect of ecological meltdown? For us, the world needed to change and it needed to change fast, but the Falklands War and the Social Democrats had helped bring Thatcher back from the brink and back into power. By the summer of 1985, the miners' strike had been defeated, Red Ken's GLC abolished and the peace movement was turning in on itself. We were losing the fight and losing badly.

Blockading bases hadn't stopped Cruise and Trident. Mass demonstrations, peace marches, peace camps, peace chains, die-ins, publicity stunts, petitions, opinion polls, letter writing, boycotts, voting, fasting, praying, singing, posters, conferences, nuclear-free councils and *even* our street theatre hadn't got rid of a single weapon! Maybe the only way to open some peoples' eyes was to put a big, fat, fucking bomb under *them*.

After five days at Hunger Hill, one of our troupe returned after a week away with some important news. Over a cup of tea, he told us about some mutual friends from Leeds who had been stopped on the A1 a few days ago because their brake lights weren't working. In the back of the friends' van was a crate of petrol bombs, destined for a department store in Sheffield that was selling fur coats.

I was not drawn to violence in defence of animal rights, but I did think that now was maybe the time for a different kind of direct action. I wasn't sure how much longer I could keep up this constant protesting that got nowhere. I was going down the road of feeling righteous fury at the world, leading me further from a sense of common humanity to the brink of political violence. I didn't want to hurt ordinary people, but I wanted people to wake up and THINK, and I wanted to wipe the smugness from the faces of the rich and powerful. And if a few of those idiots who kept them in power through laziness, greed or stupidity got hurt, maybe that served them right. Maybe now was the time for a new Angry Brigade, prepared to take on the state with the violence it was so good at using itself.

I blurted out: 'You know what makes me so fucking angry? When I was winning the Economics prize at school and getting into Oxford, it was like everyone was saying, 'Wow you're really clever'. As soon as I used that cleverness to criticise the system it was, 'Don't be so ridiculous you don't know what you're talking about'. They sent me to fucking church every week, but when I was inspired by Jesus's teaching, they told me not to be a fucking extremist. 'Don't rock the boat, you'll grow up and understand one day.' The miners' strike was our big chance, you know, but we fucking lost. Just like in 1926, the fucking sell-out union leaders with their fat salaries wouldn't support the strikers. As for the useless fucking Labour Party and of course the fucking BBC and all the fucking newspapers – they told lies all the fucking time. Thatcher used the police like her own private fucking army, and too many ordinary fucking people thought it wasn't anything to do with them. When they do realise, if they ever fucking realise, it will be too fucking late…'

There was a lengthy silence as the group digested this rare show of anger and distress from me. I usually held it in and came across as affable and amenable whilst the feelings festered deep down. Neil – thin, short, quiet and a dedicated dope-smoker – started to go through the comforting ritual of rolling a joint. He finished, lit it, took a long satisfying drag and said: 'Does anyone actually ever take any notice of anything we're saying?'

The question hung in the air, unwelcome, like a fart at a vicar's tea party. All of us wanted to believe that someone, somewhere was taking some notice of what we were doing and of what we were saying.

Fig. 18. Some of my Anarchist badges

Every day was a constant battle for self-esteem. Although I made out that I didn't care what the world thought of me, I really did want to be approved of. I wanted to be respected, to be listened to, to be heard – just like anyone else. I wanted to be able to be myself, but also to be valued as part of society. I had a lot to offer to society but no obvious ways or means of doing so. Humans are profoundly social animals and we rely on our fellow human beings for our basic sustenance, all our material needs and our emotional and intellectual existence. When I started down the road of protest and struggle for change, I had absolutely no idea how powerful this feeling of isolation from society would be, and how much pain it would cause me. These feelings had pushed me towards a hatred of society which, coupled with despair at the failure of our movements and the still burning sense of urgency for disarmament, led me to a very dark place.

25

Is There an Alternative?

Becoming more extreme and contemplating political violence was one possibility for me. The other – harder, less glamorous and more elusive – option was to find a way back into mainstream society. I had a deep fear of violence and, as a rule, I turned my anger inwards and it manifested itself as depression rather than aggression against others. I was also very lucky to have the positive influence of three strong, loving, older women in my life: my Gran in Oxford, my Mum and Amanda's mother Mary had much in common. They had all worked hard in ordinary jobs and had raised families in sometimes straightened circumstances, but they all had always found time and energy to help other people. This was done quietly and without fanfare, but still making the world a better place. I couldn't honestly say that people like this, who also loved me, were part of the problem. I couldn't reject people like these three as enemies of the revolution, even though my Mum and Gran still voted Conservative, as had Mary for most of her life. My radical views also owed more to the Sermon on the Mount than Mao's *Little Red Book*. I hadn't found a faith group that I felt I could join, but my spiritual yearnings were still strong, and I wanted to stay true to what I thought were the vital Christian teachings of love and peace.

Violence was not, therefore, a viable option for me; rather, the thought of it was an expression of my extreme frustration and anger. I also could not continue to be a full-time unpaid peace activist due to the severe lack of material resources and the wearing down of my emotional energy. After a full year of wall-to-wall protest, it was autumn again and time to work hard on our allotments and to try and find a way of making a living. I had suffered for a few years with psoriasis and joint pains as well as over-tiredness and depression. This had led me to an interest in alternative medicine. Through friends in the Green movement, I had been introduced to homeopathic medicine and had travelled down from Bradford to Sheffield to see a doctor who also practiced homeopathy. Despite the limited success of the treatment, I became fascinated by the subject. I discovered a college offering training in homeopathy in Newcastle. I applied and was accepted on a four-year part-time course staring in late September 1985.

This entailed one weekend a month in Newcastle and plenty of study at home. I had enough money saved to pay the first year's fees and asked Mum and Dad for a loan for the future years. They agreed to help, and actually paid all the fees and didn't ask for them back, for which I remain extremely grateful. For the first year I got a coach from Ripon to Sunderland, which ran once a day and took several hours. I spent three nights on the floor of my friend Steve's house – a back-to-back in Sunderland. (I had met Steve in August on the North Yorkshire peace march.) I made enough sandwiches to last the whole weekend – they were dry and unappetising by Sunday – and fed myself beans on toast for an evening meal.

Back home, a typical day would start with me, heavy-eyed from a late night, trying to appear fast asleep. Amanda was not so easily fooled. 'Wake up.' She'd made me tea. 'Bishopton today, I think. There's stuff to pick and the beans need watering.'

We had two allotments. One was an enormous, traditional plot on a council site. It's hard to believe now but, back in the mid-1980s, Amanda caused something of a stir by being a woman – and a young one at that – working on an allotment. The other plot holders were mainly old blokes who'd been doing it for years, plus a few old hippies who caught the back-to-the-land bug in the 1970s. We were the youngest by a good twenty years.

The unofficial boss was Bob Luty, a short, scrawny man in his 60s, who since retirement had expanded his empire from one to three plots, all tamed and standing to attention in neat straight lines. Weeds and pests of all kinds were attacked with manic fervour. When we started reclaiming our plot from the waist high weeds and instigated our organic methods, he would often stand and watch for a good twenty minutes, in silence. One of us would crack first: 'Hello Bob, how are you? We're planting our leeks out, what do you think?'

'Well… yer can do it like that… but I've allus thought that a nice straight row meks it easier to weed.'

Our second plot, at Bishopton, was a good half hour's walk from home. It was worth the walk to arrive at this magical place. The parcel of land consisted of around eight acres situated alongside Ripon's second, and much smaller, river. Among the tangle of trees and long undisturbed undergrowth were remnants of mill races dug by the monks of Fountains Abbey in the Middle Ages. It was a lush and tranquil plot to work, but hard graft. We had to push a wheelbarrow, or carry all the tools we thought we might need, for half an hour each way. Then there was no running water, so we had to haul buckets up the slippery riverbank and carry them a hundred yards to the thirsty vegetables.

For this day's expedition, I'd made sturdy sandwiches and we set off at midday with buckets, watering cans, hoes, forks and bags for produce. Arriving at the plot, I noticed a sudden movement behind the Jerusalem artichokes. 'What's that?'

Amanda, who was closer, shouted back: 'It's a bloody great goat eating our spinach.'

We opened the gate and there was a large white goat with tell-tale bits of green in its teeth.

'You greedy bastard! That was our dinner,' I roared.

The allotment was completely fenced in and the goat must have jumped over it to get in. It was now ducking its head and skittering around as we approached, waving our arms, clapping and shouting. This provoked our quarry to run around in circles whilst we failed to shepherd it out of the gate. This went on for a good five minutes and we were feeling foolish as well as angry. Luckily, the goat finally leapt back over the fence and away.

I had always enjoyed growing vegetables, but I learnt some valuable lessons whilst cultivating these two plots, that had a combined size of well over 600 square yards. First and foremost, I learnt that living an ecologically sustainable lifestyle is bloody hard work! The soil on the council site was good loam. This was great for the cultivation of vegetables, but also an ideal habitat for weeds. Any allotment site always has at least one plot that gets left untouched for the season, and weeds of all sorts flourish, flower and then seed. The wind does its job and thousands of new seeds land on your lovely receptive soil. Organic weed control is backbreaking work – there really is nothing romantic about the life of a peasant.

It wasn't safe to leave tools at either site because of sporadic thefts and arson attacks, so walking to the plots and carrying all the tools was extra work. We collected leaves from the streets to make leaf mould, but hours of labour only produced handfuls of lovely dark compost some two years later. It was impossible to source enough organic material to mulch more than a tiny part of the allotment, and so we bought trailer loads of farmyard manure that had to be wheel-barrowed from the road entrance and then forked in. We pissed in a bucket and carried it to the compost heap to accelerate the de-composition process. We collected the wood-ash from our fire for the same purpose. We made organic poisons from boiling rhubarb leaves for the highly toxic oxalic acid, and soaked Amanda's Mum's fag-ends in a bucket to make equally dangerous nicotine spray, both to kill aphids.

We battled against rabbits, pigeons, other birds, stray goats, slugs, snails, black fly, carrot fly, white fly, cabbage root fly, cabbage white butterflies, potato blight, weeds and the weather.

We were vegetarian, bordering on vegan, at this time. Our diet consisted of large quantities of my homemade wholemeal bread, muesli and porridge, masses of vegetables from the allotments –up to ten or twelve different types in season in one meal – and a wide variety of pulses bought from the local wholefood shop. These were accompanied by brown rice by the bucketful, miso, tahini, peanut butter, vegetable pate, tofu, soya milk and desserts and a small quantity of free-range eggs, cheese, and milk for tea. I made beer from kits and wine from elderberries and elderflowers, blackberries, parsnips and rhubarb. We bought nearly all our groceries from the wholefood shop in town – where Amanda had worked as a Saturday girl when she was still at school – out of the £14 a week we put aside for food. We lived on supplementary benefit of just under £40 a week for the two of us.[4] We gave £14 of that to Amanda's Mum towards the utility bills, put £14 in the kitty for food and had £12 to spend on everything else.

Our main source of heating was a log fire in the living room. We gathered wood and I sawed it up on a homemade sawhorse and carried it to the top of the three-storey house. We didn't drive, and anyway couldn't possibly have afforded a car, so we walked, cycled and hitch-hiked everywhere, with the occasional bus or train ride.

---

[4] Worth between £100-140 today, depending on the method of calculation.

There were no mobile phones or computers, I didn't have a camera or a television and we couldn't afford the cinema. So, for entertainment we made do with a radio-cassette player, books and the odd visit to the pub. We wore second-hand clothes, swam in the River Ure as well as the local pool, and cycled in the Dales.

I was now studying for up to twenty hours a week on the homeopathy course, but this became difficult as the winter took hold. I discovered that when the temperature drops to a certain level, you cannot keep warm, no matter how many clothes you put on. I would settle down to study my homoeopathic Materia Medica. The first hour would be all right, then a hot drink and a bit of jumping around would get me through the second. Then I just got too cold to concentrate. I measured the temperature and discovered that anything below 15°C made studying very difficult, and when it got to 12°C, you may as well give up before you start...

I had great hopes that homoeopathy would in time provide me with the opportunity for meaningful, useful work and income. It was, however, going to be several years before I could hope to make any money from it, rather than spending on books, remedies and travelling to the course. Amanda and I were also keen to find our own place to live. Her parents had been very kind, but we wanted to try and make our own life together away from Ripon. One possible solution to both our needs of work and somewhere to live was joining a commune that involved making a living as an integral part of the setup. My experiences with the Teachers in North Wales hadn't put me off the idea completely, and the Catholic Worker Housing in Kansas City had given me a much more positive experience of shared living and working. We sent off for the directory of 'intentional communities' as they were called, and placed a small ad in *Peace News*. Over the summer of 1986 we visited five possible places.

The adventure started with a letter from Bruce in Fife, who had seen our advert. He was trying to establish a viable smallholding with communal accommodation. We hitched up the A1 from Ripon and arrived in rural Fife in time for tea, which included delicious courgette-flower fritters, made by a young Italian lad who was Bruce's only other helper at the time. We received a warm welcome from our host, but that was the only warm thing about the place!

170

The next day I spent six hours weeding an onion field in the rain. This crushed any lingering idealistic dreams I had of living off the land using organic methods. I had worked hard and had the backache to prove it, but I had only got through about a fifth of the field. If I'd been paid, even a minimum wage, those onions would have been the most expensive in Scotland. The next day was even wetter and was spent cleaning and sorting tools in an outbuilding, which at least gave me some satisfaction, as I had taken on my Dad's love of looking after garden tools properly. We hitched back to Ripon after a thanks-but-no-thanks chat with the forlorn Bruce.

I made two visits to an inspirational organisation called Delos in Wellingborough. This was a community set up by a couple who wanted to create a place for people with special needs (who at the time were referred to as 'mentally-handicapped') to live alongside more able adults. There were two large houses, three small ones, several large allotments and a wholefood shop. They were looking for a couple to run one of the small houses. An added attraction was that one of the founders, Jeanne, had been very involved in the peace movement at the nearby Molesworth base.

I was drawn to the Christian basis of the community and I liked the town. Nothing fancy, but cosy to live in – big enough to have facilities but small enough to walk around. Amanda, however, exercised her veto on joining this community. I was disappointed at the time, but looking back I think she was probably right. She hated anything that smacked of religion and this would have caused conflict with me and others in the community.

Parsonage Farm started as a classic 1970s 'big house in the country' commune, but unlike most others it prospered financially. Some of the core members had started a successful technology company, and this would have been perfect had there been an opening for us to work in the business. It was a workers' co-operative making intermediate technology products for agriculture in the developing world. Sadly, there were no vacancies at the time. What was on offer was a lovely, well-maintained place to live in the countryside near Cambridge, plus pocket money, in return for domestic duties: sort of live-in servants, who were nominally equal. This was problematic, especially as the core group of six adults included two brothers and their wives and children, but we were on the verge of accepting their offer to move in for a trial period in September 1986. We were getting desperate, and there were fabulous gardens here along with goats, chickens and bees as well as friendly people, a warm comfortable house and a long way from Ripon and our past life.

In between visits to Parsonage Farm in sunny Cambridgeshire, we went to the only completely shared wealth-and-income commune on our list, and possibly the only one in the country at the time apart from the Teachers. It was called Lifespan and was everything the Teachers in North Wales wasn't. It was genuinely democratic and equal and not weird at all. Ideologically, this was exactly what I believed in: people living and working together as equals. The commune was situated in the far South West of Yorkshire, in the foothills of the Pennines. The members ran a small printing business and some of them worked outside and pooled their income. There were also other potential business opportunities using the spare out-buildings. The original members had bought a row of ex-railway workers' terraced houses and land when the shunting yard nearby closed. There were no near neighbours and the views were dominated by the treeless, black Pennines on the skyline.

The people were friendly, and they had created magnificently productive organic vegetable plots. These were, however, very weedy and the communal areas indoors were crying out for a good clean. It was cold and slightly damp in the living room and the random collection of sofas and armchairs and stained beige carpet were not enticing. It was also clear that there was some tension between some of the members. When, over a bottle of beer in the kitchen that evening, we were regaled with stories of nocturnal visits from biker gangs looking to smash something up, my ideological fervour waned. I loved the idea of this community, but the reality of this glowering bleak landscape brought me down. The lack of care for the communal areas and the bubbling tensions in the community also illustrated the gap between idealism and reality.

After much agonising, we eventually turned down the offer from Parsonage farm. To be honest, I think it just felt too risky and too far from any friends and support networks. The next year was then, however, one of mounting desperation to get out of Ripon and off the dole. It had been at least six months since we had been down to Oxford. We hitched down in late August to stay with Gran and

Auntie Pinkie (who had now moved in with her twin). We lined up visits to all our old friends and to my ninety-year-old godmother, Auntie Hilda. Before we set off, Gran happened to mention that Hilda's daughter, June, was worried that her mum was alone in her house after a long-term lodger had moved out in the spring. Hilda didn't feel confident enough to take in a stranger, nor did she want to be bothered with upgrading the accommodation. Amanda and I had the same thought at the same time. Why not move down to Oxford? Work would be much easier to find, the weather was better, and we had a support network in place. We spoke to June and Hilda and they were delighted at the prospect. This felt like Providence. Within two weeks, our ever-faithful friend and removal-man-in-chief Mark had moved us down to Oxford in his van, bringing not only our belongings and bikes, but also bags of well-rotted compost and leaf-mould that were just too precious to leave behind.

26
A New Jerusalem?

The day after we arrived in Oxford we went down to the Job Centre and signed up for the new government Enterprise Allowance scheme, which was an encouragement for the long-term unemployed to start their own businesses. You had to put £1,000 in a business bank account and in return you would receive some basic business training and £40 a week for a year. My homeopathy course included provision for students to start treating clients under supervision, once they were at least in the third year and had completed the practical training. This mostly consisted of sitting in with experienced professionals, observing them at work and then discussing the cases. In Oxford, I found a willing practitioner and was able to complete this training at the same time that the Enterprise Allowance business training finished in late October. I immediately paid a visit to a print shop on the Cowley Road and used my first business cheque to pay for letterheads and business cards, and prepared to launch my new career.

Auntie Hilda lived on Divinity Road, part of a late-Victorian/Edwardian development that was grander than the terraced streets filling up the East Oxford triangles between the Cowley Road and the Iffley Road and St. Clements. Hilda had married into a family that had run river boats on the Thames, and well into her fifties she swam daily in the river. Unfortunately, her husband died relatively young and she was left to bring up her daughter, June, on her own. She was a hugely determined woman who turned her hand to various business ventures and took in lodgers in order to keep her house. By the time we moved in with her, she was living downstairs except for a weekly bath upstairs. She had put on some weight by this time and each week, when bath time approached, I would keep my fingers crossed that she would get out without difficulty, as I dreaded having to rescue her from the tub. I did have to pick her up off the floor once and it was like lifting a sack of cement. The front room upstairs was the best in the house, with wide bay windows and the morning sun. However, it was not for us as it had been devoted to the over-wintering of Hilda's impressive geranium collection. We had to make do with a decent-sized but gloomy bedroom, a galley kitchen and a small lounge at the back of the house, which did benefit from the afternoon and evening sun. The window afforded a view over the lush neighbouring gardens with their well-kept lawns, laurel hedges, lilacs and flowering cherries. The switch for the immersion heater was in Hilda's snug downstairs and she guarded the allocation of hot water with the zeal of a wartime bureaucrat in charge of petrol-rationing. We were, however, grateful for the modest rent that was the other side of the equation.

The location proved advantageous to Amanda, who had chosen to set herself up as a domestic cleaner under the Enterprise Allowance scheme. We only had to leaflet the three adjacent streets once for her to get almost a full week of work. I also picked up a couple of gardening and cleaning jobs myself to get some cash flowing in.

I couldn't use the house for my practice though, and so I had to look for somewhere to rent. I was lucky that a new development had just been completed that linked Oxford's atmospheric covered market with Cornmarket Street, the main pedestrianised shopping street. It was on the site of a mediaeval inn called the Golden Cross. The result was a secret courtyard surrounded by half-timbered buildings that now housed shops and restaurants. One of these shops was Neal's Yard, an offshoot from the original in Covent Garden. It sold ethical cosmetics and alternative remedies, and above the shop was a consulting room that I was able to rent one day a week for a share of any fees I received.

On my first day as a professional homeopath, I got off the bus at the top of the high street and walked through the Victorian cast-iron gates of the covered market. The heart of the market was blessed with dappled sun from a lofty skylight, and the echoing clatter of feet on the concrete floor joined the chorus of buying and selling. My Gran, Grandad and Auntie Pinkie had all worked a few days a week in a newsagent's in this market after they had retired from running their shop on the Cowley Road, and I had enjoyed visiting them there as a boy. This gave me an extra reason to love this special place. There was also the appetising smell of coffee being ground, long before coffee-shops sprang up on every corner. I walked all the way through the market to Neal's Yard and entered the shop accompanied by the tinkle of the doorbell. In the softly lit, wood-dominated space, the everyday smells of the market were replaced by an almost overpowering scent of sweet soaps and perfumes. The gentle New Age music and the subtle lighting created a calm and dreamlike feeling. Any minute now, a real-live human being could be coming to me for treatment, I thought, as I mounted the highly-polished wooden stairs.

I had to be careful not to slip in my new shiny-leather Loakes. They were the first proper shoes that I had worn after at least six years of trainers or boots. I had found them in a sale, but they were still expensive, all-leather, made-in-England shoes. I needed to mark my transformation from unemployed peace activist to professional homeopathic practitioner. I didn't really have the wardrobe to match the shoes, but I had cut my hair and shaved my beard off and, along with new cords and an ironed shirt, I was unrecognisable from six months ago.

This momentous Tuesday was a sunny, mellow late autumn day. I didn't actually have any clients yet and I spent a long time sitting at the small table in the sloping-floored room, looking out of the window. My imagination wandered between picturing this place as the bustling mediaeval inn it once was, to the last time I was in Oxford as a student, to the future when my name would be proudly displayed on a brass plate outside, a steady stream of grateful clients would climb these ancient stairs and I would have a decent income earned from my own efforts.

Obviously, it was going to take some time to build up a client base and I didn't want to be doing more than a day a week gardening and cleaning (think of my hands) for extra money. Luckily, my old friend, Ecology Party stalwart and bookshop owner Jon came to my rescue. Times were changing in Britain in the late 1980s. The explosion of political unrest that I had been sucked into had been replaced by an acceptance of neoliberal political dominance, with Mrs Thatcher winning a third general election. This spawned the phenomenon of yuppies, the enterprise culture and a growing focus on the individual rather than the collective. This was a disaster for the sales of radical political books, and Jon's shop was failing fast. He was in the process of winding down the business and starting a new Green publishing venture. He needed someone to mind the shop a few days a week and field the many calls asking for money. I reassured everyone that their cheque really was in the post, or soon would be, sold a few books and postcards and read a lot of the New Age twaddle that was now selling like hot cakes.

Gradually I gained a handful of clients for my homeopathy, but not enough to do more than cover basic costs. I organised and taught a series of evening classes on using homeopathy at home and found that I was better at this than the actual practice of healing.

Then, on Thursday 16 October, my worst fears seemed to have materialised. We had slept long and deeply and, as I woke and realised that it was well after 9 am, I fumbled for the radio to blast us awake with Radio 1. Instead of the latest hits, I heard a sombre voice talking about power outages and transport meltdowns. In my semi-somnolent state, I felt a cold chill through my whole body, and I shivered uncontrollably. This was it. Someone had misread the signs and fired a nuclear weapon in error. This could be the beginning of nuclear Armageddon. So, it was going to end like this, just when we were starting to make a fresh start... I couldn't bear to think what was happening outside, so I hid my head under the covers, clutched my soft-toy hedgehog to my chest and prayed for deliverance. I slipped into a half-awake, half-asleep state with terrifying dreams of melting human faces. The radio burbled on, and as I woke up properly, I heard another news bulletin that made it clear that what had actually happened was an unprecedented powerful storm that had wreaked havoc all around us as we slept on, oblivious.

The emotional toll of the last eight years had been heavy. I had made a sudden and extreme split from my family expectations and support systems. I had deliberately put myself on the fringes of society and struggled physically and emotionally with the consequences. I had become aware of the cruelties and deep iniquities of the world, and despite my complete commitment and dedicated efforts, had been unable to change anything. This brought with it a burden of knowledge and despair. Like many people before and after me, I now sought out the support of a faith community to seek the spiritual solace I needed after this failure to establish a peaceful heaven-on-earth.

I had been brought up in the Christian tradition and had been profoundly influenced as a teenager by Jesus's teachings, but like many young people, I had rebelled against the established Church. I had, though, never lost an emotional pull towards spirituality, but like many other people I found organised religion and dogmatic faiths difficult to reconcile with my intellectual and political beliefs. I had tried a Quaker meeting in my first term at Bradford, but after hooking up with Amanda, a confirmed and virulent atheist, I had kept away from churches of all kinds. I continued to meet Quakers and other radical Christians through the peace movement, and was influenced by Tony Smith in particular, Amanda's old art teacher, stalwart of Ripon for Peace, good friend to us both and a Quaker. This new start gave me the opportunity to give religion a try. The Society of Friends, or Quakers, with their famous Peace Testimony and disregard for authority, were an obvious first choice.

Quakerism, along with a range of other radical religious and political groups, emerged in the seventeenth century during the period of civil war and massive social, political and religious upheaval. However, once Cromwell had crushed the Levellers at Burford and pressed the New Model Army into laying waste to parts of Ireland, political radicalism was cowed and ultimately defeated. Groups such as the Diggers and the Ranters faded away into exile, madness, prison or back into conformity. The Restoration of Charles the Second led to a modicum of religious toleration though, and the Quakers were allowed to survive as long as they distanced themselves from political dissidents and focussed on private religious practice, which they did.

I had learnt this history over a period of two years of WEA evening classes in Harrogate whilst on the dole in Ripon, but it was only much later that I saw how closely my own experience matched that of the seventeenth-century radicals. A period of significant political and social upheaval allowed what otherwise might have been only radical thoughts to find expression in action. Like George Fox, the founder of Quakerism, I was also just emerging into adulthood as this time of upheaval began. The common dissatisfaction young adults have with current orthodoxies were magnified by the times. A large-enough movement, or counterculture, grew up to nourish individuals and also to challenge them to take risks and dream the improbable.

To begin with, everything seemed possible and, as cracks appeared in the systems and structures of power and control, a New Jerusalem could be glimpsed. Then the system, the state, the powers that be, fought back. The movement could not present a united front and individuals and groups were picked off one-by-one by the authorities, and the dream faded. Some radicals were crushed, physically or mentally. Others, nimbler and less ideologically-rigid, re-invented themselves and shed their radical past, like a snake shedding its skin. Others still, like the Quakers once did, eschewed politics and turned inwards to seek liberation through religious experience.

The Quaker Meeting House in Oxford was situated on the ancient thoroughfare of St Giles, near the monument commemorating the sixteenth-century protestant martyrs who had been burned at the stake. The building itself had wooden structures that dated back to at least the seventeenth century and probably earlier. On the Sunday immediately after the storm and my waking terrors, I got up earlier than usual, left Amanda sleeping, and cycled into town. I locked my bike to a lamppost outside the Meeting House and nervously walked through the heavy oak door. I discovered that a new meeting room had been built in the garden of the original property. I sucked deep on the autumn air, a mix of decay and fecundity, as I walked up the lichen-patinaed path on the start of my journey to what, I hoped, would be inner peace after the turmoil and despair of the last eight years. There were at least forty people in the room as my first meeting started. I sat in a corner, closed my eyes and tried to connect to the deepening silence.

Epilogue

22 April 2019 – Waterloo Bridge

U nlike so many of the sit-down protests I've written about in
this book, the Extinction Rebellion (XR) blockade of several
London Bridges and Oxford Circus was blessed with warm sunshine. I had agonised for weeks over whether to go and support
the activists. This was the first time in the UK since February 1986
– when 6,000 of us blockaded the Molesworth cruise missile base in
Cambridgeshire – that thousands of people had turned to civil disobedience in the face of an existential threat to human life on earth.

Most of the people I could see on the bridge would not have been
born in 1986 and almost certainly knew nothing of our struggle. I
am no longer the hairy young rebel dressed in a random collection
of free clothes. My hair is thinning, my neatly-trimmed beard is
grey, and my ordinary shirt and trousers are straining to hold in my
expansive middle-aged spread. I feel a gulf between myself and the
young protesters. I'm actually a bit jealous of their smooth youthful
faces, shining with hope and righteousness. Not only have they been
lucky with the weather, but by the standards of the 1980s the police
are being extraordinary restrained and courteous. Despite the travel
chaos they are causing ordinary Londoners, XR are getting a fair
amount of public support too. Greta Thunberg is in town talking to
our politicians and David Attenborough has come off the fence and
produced a programme that tells Middle England about the reality
of the severe climate crisis. Can I dare to hope sufficiently in order to
take this sort of action again? Because that is what it takes. It is hope
rather than despair that drives popular uprisings. There is of course
plenty of fear about what might happen to us in the future, but fear
on its own tends to lead to disengagement. It is the hope of creating
a better world that spurs people to action. After forty years of trying
to change the world, my supplies of hope have dwindled.

Homeopathy and Quakerism did transform my life, but not in
the ways that I had imagined. Despite consulting some of the most

eminent homeopaths in the country, my own health problems were never helped. And although I had trained for four years and tried my best, I never gained enough clients to even cover my costs – and I'm not at all sure that I helped any of the clients that came to see me. I wasn't a natural healer and I now question whether homeopathic medicines really work. However, I started teaching evening classes in homeopathic first aid, and took an Open University course on Health and Disease in 1988. I realised that I was a much better teacher than healer, and that the Open University model worked well for me. By October 1992, I had an Open University degree and a place on the PGCE course at Leeds University to become a secondary school Economics teacher.

In the meantime, Amanda and I had bought a very cheap one-bedroom flat in the Scottish Borders, with substantial help from my Mum and Dad. We continued to live a low-impact and sustainable lifestyle. I planted fruit trees in our small back garden, started cultivating a piece of wasteland to grow vegetables on, collected firewood for our fire, washed the clothes in the bath, ate a wholefood vegetarian diet, walked and cycled, and had another go at practising homeopathy and re-joined the Green Party. Our relationship was failing, however, and although it took more than two years' of break-ups and reunions, we finally ended our eleven years together at the end of 1993.

Quaker meetings had been a great comfort during this emotionally traumatic time, but the greatest gift has not been spiritual strength, but meeting my wife Margie in 1994 at a Quaker event in London. We married a year later at the Hammersmith Meeting and are fast approaching our Silver wedding anniversary, still lucky to be very happy together. Marrying Margie has given me financial security and has blessed me with terrific stepchildren, discovering the joy of Irish Terriers, musical theatre, partner dancing and the Racing Demon card game. I am a very lucky man.

Getting my first full-time career job at the age of 32 was a shock to my system. Working in schools (which are essentially rule-bound, conservative places) after having been so far outside mainstream society for a dozen years, was perhaps a similar experience to soldiers returning from war to civvy street. I didn't feel that I could talk to my colleagues, students or the people I met socially about the last twelve years of my life, because it would have made no sense to them. It was particularly ironic that I ended up having to teach a lot of Business Studies as fewer and fewer students were taking Economics.

After six years, this identity crisis, coupled with resentment at being junior to younger and less academically-able colleagues, plus the normal strains for teachers of long hours, unmotivated students, constantly changing curricula and exam specifications – and finally OFSTED – landed me on a therapist's couch and then in the doctor's surgery, being prescribed antidepressants. I managed to finish a part-time MA and worked in educational research and teacher training (mostly part-time because of my growing health problems) for another thirteen years. Among other things, I was involved in promoting and reforming Vocational Education, the 16-19 curriculum and Education for Sustainability. All these initiatives were squashed by government policy.

The education sector has not been a happy place to work since the 1988 and 1992 reforms and the subsequent establishment of quasi-markets. The rise to dominance of managerialism as an approach to organising the workplace has had a profoundly negative impact on the work-lives of many people. The combination of marketisation and managerialism has led to constant change and disruption, and an undermining of the professional status of teachers and educationalists in general, unstable employment and an increase in power for the employer. The combination of funding imperatives, terror through inspection regimes, judgement by quantitative results, and systems of appraisal and self-regulation have combined to impose an ideological straitjacket on workers. I found very little room to oppose the dominant ideology.

By now, Margie and I had moved to Dorset, where we had holidayed every year since we met. I thought it would solve all my problems, moving to a beautiful place with plenty of more relaxed, alternative types around. Unfortunately, I hadn't realised that I would be bringing myself with me. I suffered a serious emotional breakdown. I was helped through by a fine therapist, Margie and good friends. But it wasn't until I started taking stronger drugs that I stabilised. Five years volunteering at Dorset Reclaim, a charity recycling furniture for the benefit of folk on low incomes, starting but not finishing a PhD in Green politics, learning the ukulele, initiating a socialist choir and regular sessions cleaning up the River Wandle are some of the activities

I've managed, despite my struggle with chronic fatigue and joint and muscle pains. I have continued to enjoy being a househusband and feel comfortable in the domestic sphere. I haven't been able to bear the silence of Quaker meetings since my breakdown but have recently started going to a warm and loving Universalist Unitarian Chapel.

I do wonder how much my activism cost me in terms of my health. My choosing of voluntary poverty and giving up the possibility of power and social status did not lead to any significant change in the world. This has been a difficult burden to bear and I've never reconciled myself to the loss of 'young successful Chris with the world at his feet'. In his very influential essay published in 1968, *Tragedy of the Commons*, Garrett Hardin put forward the idea that people are prone to pursue private benefit, even if it conflicts with a wider social/human interest. For example, most people are very unlikely to make a choice based on public interest, such as *not* having children because of the population explosion, or *not* flying because of the threat of climate change. The solution to this, according to Hardin, is to develop some kind of mutually agreed mutual coercion. People who do follow their conscience and forego things they would like, suffer 'Pathogenic Effects of Conscience', according to Hardin:

> The long-term disadvantage of an appeal to conscience should be enough to condemn it; but it has serious short-term disadvantages as well. If we ask a man who is exploiting, to desist 'in the name of conscience' what are we saying to him? What does he hear? Not only at the moment but also in the wee small hours of night when, after sleep, he remembers not merely the words we use but also the non-verbal communication cues we gave him unawares? Sooner or later, consciously, he senses that he has received two communications, and that they are contradictory: 1) the intended communication, 'if you don't do as we ask people openly condemn you for not acting like a responsible citizen'; 2) the unintended indication; 'if you do behave as we ask, we will secretly condemn you to a simpleton who can be shamed into standing aside while the rest of us exploit the commons... Everyman is then caught in what Bateson has called a double bind. Bateson and his co-workers have made

Fig. 19. All my old badges

a plausible case for viewing the double bind as an important causative factor in the genesis of schizophrenia. The double bind may not always be so damaging, but it always endangers the mental health of anyone to whom it is applied.[5]

---

[5] Garrett Hardin: 'The Tragedy of the Commons', *Science*, 13 Dec 1968: Vol. 162, Issue 3859, pp. 1243-1248.

Back on Waterloo Bridge, I find myself pouring my story out to a young woman who gives me a leaflet about the protest. She seems to be really listening and showing concern and respect. I step over the barrier from the public pavement into the part occupied by the protesters. I'm not ready to sit down for hours or be removed by the police, but I am able to identify myself as a rebel and show solidarity for an hour or two. It turns out that it's not so easy to extinguish that flame of hope. As the crisis deepens, I know which side I'm on.

Books to challenge  *your perception of reality*

A message from Clairview

We are an independent publishing company with a focus on cutting-edge, non-fiction books. Our innovative list covers current affairs and politics, health, the arts, history, science and spirituality. But regardless of subject, our books have a common link: they all question conventional thinking, dogmas and received wisdom.

Despite being a small company, our list features some big names, such as Booker Prize winner Ben Okri, literary giant Gore Vidal, world leader Mikhail Gorbachev, modern artist Joseph Beuys and natural childbirth pioneer Michel Odent.

So, check out our full catalogue online at
www.clairviewbooks.com
and join our emailing list for news on new titles.

office@clairviewbooks.com

CLAIRVIEW